POLITICAL SCIENCE AND HISTORY

SMART DEVELOPMENT

THE POLITICAL ECONOMY IN A POST-COVID-19 WORLD

POLITICAL SCIENCE AND HISTORY

Additional books and e-books in this series can be found on Nova's website under the Series tab.

POLITICAL SCIENCE AND HISTORY

SMART DEVELOPMENT

THE POLITICAL ECONOMY IN A POST-COVID-19 WORLD

ARNO TAUSCH

nova science publishers
New York

NOTICE TO THE READER

Library of Congress Cataloging-in-Publication Data

ISBN: 978-1-53619-379-4

Published by Nova Science Publishers, Inc. † New York

CONTENTS

PREFACE

In this book, we present a first empirical reflection on 'smart development', its measurement and its possible 'drivers' and 'bottlenecks'. With the hitherto existing globalized political economy in ruins in the wake of the Covid-19 pandemic and the ensuing global economic depression, a new societal contract has to emerge which combines well-being with a minimum of energy inputs.

This very idea of 'smart development' was first proposed by Meadows (1992) and has not been really followed up to now in social science ever since. We first provide cross-national data, how much ecological footprint is used in the nations of the world system to 'deliver' a given amount of democracy, economic growth, gender equality, human development, research and development, and social cohesion. To this end, we first developed UNDP-type performance indicators from current standard international comparative, cross-national social science data on these six main dimensions of development and on the combined performance on the six dimensions (a UNDP type 'human development index plus'). We then show the non-linear standard OLS regression trade-offs between ecological footprints per capita and their square on these six components of development and the overall super-UNDP development performance index, derived from them. The residuals from these regressions are our new measures of smart development: a country experiences smart development, if it achieves a maximum of democracy, economic growth, gender equality, human development, research and development, and social cohesion, and the combination of them with a minimum of ecological footprint.

We then look at the cross-national drivers and bottlenecks of this 'smart development', using standard comparative cross-national data, which operationalize standard economic, sociological and political science knowledge in international development accounting. We compare the predictive power of these standard predictors, using standard OLS stepwise regression procedures, based on IBM SPSS XXIV. Apart from important variables and indicators, derived from sociological dependency and world systems theories, we also test the predictive power of other predictors as well, ranging from geography and achieved development levels to the clash of civilization models, feminist theories, migration theories, and the 'small is beautiful paradigm' in the tradition of Schumacher. Our estimates underline the enormous importance of the transfer of resources from the centre to the periphery, brought about by migration, with huge statistical observed positive effects of received worker remittances on smart human development, Happy Life Years, smart gender justice, smart R&D, and both formulations of the smart development index.

Finally, we take up an issue, which has been very prominent in recent global public health debate. Following the path-breaking articles by R. G. Wilkinson and associates, income inequality has a very detrimental effect on life quality. But life quality also depends in a non-linear fashion from environmental data. Thus, the Wilkinson research agenda finds its proper place also in debates about 'smart development', but certainly, the weight of other variables, such as

- Membership in the Islamic Conference
- military expenditures per GDP
- Muslim population share per total population
- public education expenditure per GNP
- UNDP education index
- worker remittance inflows as % of GDP

also has to be properly taken into account.

JEL Classification

C43 - Index Numbers and Aggregation

Q56 - Environment and Development; Environment and Trade; Sustainability; Environmental Accounts and Accounting; Environmental Equity; Population Growth

F22 - International Migration

F-24 - Remittances

INTRODUCTION

In this book, we present a first empirical reflection on *'smart development'*, and its measurement and its possible 'drivers' and 'bottlenecks'. The very idea of *'smart development'*, now at the beginning of a global economic depression in the wake of the Covid-19 pandemic, was first proposed by Meadows (1992) and has not been really followed up to now in social science ever since. In the face of the huge usage of this term in the international media, such a statement is perhaps surprising, but our verdict corresponds to the clear bibliographical evidence on the base of such indices as *'Web of Knowledge'* or *'Scopus'*.

The basic idea, proposed by Meadows three decades ago in his pioneering article on the issue was that we should relate our whole concept of development, and not just economic growth, to the natural resources needed to sustain it. In a similar vein, the Happy Planet Organization presented the so-called 'Happy Planet Index' (HPI), which is, as it is perhaps known to the readership of this publication, an index of measuring the trade-off between ecological footprint data and life quality (Happy Life Years, HLYE). Arguably, ecological footprint today is the best single international yardstick for environmental destruction in a nation (see also York, Rosa, and Dietz, 2003).

Economic theory, for sure, is conscious about the non-linearity of the trade-off between income and happiness, with rising income levels not necessarily increasing the happiness of all. This phenomenon has become widely known in the economic research literature as the *'Easterlin paradoxon'* (Easterlin, 1995, 2001; Frey and Stutzer, 2002; Oswald, 1997; Stevenson and Wolfers, 2007). But here, we provide the first cross-national data, how much ecological footprint is used in the nations of the world system to 'deliver' a given amount of democracy, economic growth, gender equality, human development, research and development, and social cohesion.

To this end, we first developed UNDP-type performance indicators from current standard international comparative, cross-national social science data on the six main dimensions of development (democracy, economic growth, gender equality, human development, research and development, and social cohesion) and on the combined performance on these six dimensions (a kind of super-UNDP *'human development index').* We then show the non-linear standard OLS regression trade-offs between ecological footprints per capita and their square on these six components of development and the overall super-UNDP development performance index, derived from them. The residuals from these regressions are our new measures of smart development: a country experiences smart development, if it achieves a maximum of democracy, economic growth, gender equality, human development, research and development, and social cohesion, and the combination of them with a minimum of ecological footprint.

We then look at the cross-national drivers and bottlenecks of this 'smart development', using standard comparative cross-national data, which operationalize standard economic, sociological and political science knowledge in international development accounting. We compare the predictive power of these standard predictors, using standard OLS stepwise regression procedures, based on IBM SPSS XXIV. Apart from important variables and indicators, derived from sociological dependency and world systems theories, we also test the predictive power of other predictors as well, ranging from geography and achieved development levels to the clash of civilization models, feminist theories, migration theories, and the *'small is beautiful paradigm'* in the tradition of Schumacher.

In Chapter 2 we sketch the theoretical background. Chapter 3 will introduce the measurement concepts and the methodology of this book. Chapter 4 will be dedicated to the presentation of the results on the drivers and bottlenecks of *'smart development',* while Chapter 5 will discuss the results in the framework of earlier theories and hitherto existing research, relevant for our subject. Chapter 6 looks into the trade-off between inequality and smart development. Chapter 7 presents our preliminary conclusions.

Chapter 1

THEORETICAL BACKGROUND AND EARLIER STUDIES

As of October 2020, we drift towards the abyss of the current recession of all global recessions in the period since the Great Depression, 1929, and the Second World War. The vulnerabilities of entire regions will increase, and crises of all sorts, state failures and conflicts will ensue.

So, what is the nature of the global recession, which we are now facing? Writing in mid-April 2020, we can safely say that events in the wake of the Covid-19 pandemic which originated from the Huanan Seafood Market in Wuhan, China are set to fatally change the fortunes of the 21st century in January 2020. As the *NY Times* showed on March 22, 2020 (see Wu, et al., 2020), thousands of people from Wuhan did not stop traveling abroad even after the Chinese authorities were aware of the serious pandemic. Not all countries reacted to the crisis with the necessary determination, like South Korea.

But already before the Covid-19 pandemic and recession, we were facing a weak and internally divided West, above all in European Union, affected by a plurality of internal and external crises, such as Brexit, the lack of real democracy at a European Union level, the malfunctioning of European monetary union and the lack of a coherent European foreign policy.

Now, last March 23, 2020 was the day which will go down in European economic history as the day on which the core of the European Union's hitherto existing neoliberal fiscal policy framework, the Maastricht criteria, were put out of action (D'Elia, 2020; on the background see also D'Elia and de Santis, 2019). The German Bundesbank, on its official website, still proudly declares that

> "sound public finances are the cornerstone of a stability-oriented monetary union. The EU Member States therefore set out fiscal rules in the Maastricht Treaty and subsequently augmented them with the Stability and Growth Pact. The Maastricht Treaty specifies reference values for the general government sector of the various EU Member States: 3% of gross domestic product (GDP) for the government deficit and 60% of GDP for government debt (the Maastricht criteria)."[1]

But all that is now history. The Maastricht criteria fixed European economic policy targets of low inflation, a low ratio of gross government debt relative to GDP at market prices below 60%, and low long-term interest rates. The International Monetary Fund now already anticipates a global recession of minus 2.9% due to the "corona crisis".[2] Serious model calculations by Warwick McKibbin and Roshen Fernando from the Australian National University (McKibbin and Fernando, 2020), expect at least 15 to 68 million global deaths from the current corona infection and a recession of over 8% in the countries of the euro zone. The current pandemic thus threatens to become the primary catastrophe of the 21st century. In their study of the 1918-1920 flu epidemic which was a similar global disaster, Johnson and Mueller, 2002, concluded that 48 million to 100 million people worldwide fell victim to the "Spanish flu" at that time. Harvard economist Robert Barro (Barro, Ursua and Weng, 2020; Barro, 2006) speaks quite logically of *"rare macroeconomic disasters"* that shake the foundations of

---

1 https://www.bundesbank.de/en/statistics/public-finances/maastricht-deficit-and-debt-level/maastricht-deficit-and-debt-level-793140.

2 https://www.imf.org/en/Topics/imf-and-covid19/Policy-Responses-to-COVID-19 and https://www.nzz.ch/wirtschaft/der-imf-erachtet-die-corona-krise-als-ernsthaftes-risiko-fuer-die-weltwirtschaft-ld.1544427.

the global economy with recurrent force and regularity. Both Johnson and Muller as well as Barro, Ursua and Weng, 2020 highlight that there is a clear north-south global differential in fatality rates, with highest fatalities to be observed in the weaker countries of the global periphery and semi-periphery.

In their comparison of the effects of the Spanish flu in 1918 and Covid-19 today, Barro, Ursua and Weng, 2020 conclude:

> "Both the implications of our findings from the Great Influenza Epidemic for the ongoing coronavirus epidemic are unsettling. (…) The flu death rate of 2.0 percent out of the (…) total population in 1918-1920 translates into 150 million deaths worldwide when applied to the world's population of around 7.5 billion in 2020. Further, this death rate corresponds in our regression analysis to declines in the typical country by 6 percent for GDP and 8 percent for consumption. These economic declines are comparable to those last seen during the global Great Recession of 2008-2009. The results also suggest substantial short-term declines in real returns on stocks and short-term government bills. Thus, the possibility exists not only for unprecedented numbers of deaths but also for major global economic dislocation. Although these outcomes for the coronavirus are only possibilities, corresponding to plausible worst-case scenarios, the large potential losses in lives and economic activity justify substantial outlays to attempt to limit the damage. However, extreme mitigation efforts—such as widespread cancellations of travel, meetings, and major events—will themselves contribute to the depressed economic activity." (Barro, Ursua and Weng, 2020)

In Europe, the nationwide victim numbers from the flu epidemic in 1918-20 have a relatively large correlation with today's corona numbers.[3] As if the susceptibility to such disasters had been dislocated forever to southern Europe! With 1.07% per total population, Egypt's death rate during the flu epidemic of 1918-20 was among the world's higher rates, and about equal to those of Austria, China, Hungary, Italy, Korea, Malaysia, Spain, and Turkey, but still lower than that of India, Indonesia, and Mexico, which were

[3] Simple Microsoft EXCEL correlations between the mentioned historical data on the Spanish flu and current covid-19 infection data, as reported in https://www.worldometers.info/coronavirus/.

at the lamentable global top. We can roughly say that a fatality rate of around 1% corresponded to the countries of what was then the semi-periphery, while higher rates were typical in the world system's periphery (as to long-run time series data of global development ranging well into the 19th Century, justifying such assumptions, see Grinin, et al., 2016).

Taubenberger and Morens, 2006 highlighted that the "Spanish flu" hit the world in three waves, with the first one in summer 1918 and a death rate of around 5 per 1.000 persons in the United Kingdom, while the deadliest, second wave occurred more than a year later in November 1918, with a death rate of around 25 per 1.000 persons, and a third peak having been reached in March, 1919, with a death rate of 10 per 1.000 persons. If that logic of death were to apply again, the current more than 1,5 million Coronavirus cases and more than 88,000 deaths recorded by April 9, 2020, 4:14 GMT,[4] will be nothing compared to the wave of death which could sweep across our globe by 2021, with five times the current rates of infection.

In this context, the Italian economist Giovanni Andrea Cornia (Cornia, 2019; Cornia and Paniccià, 2000) has proven that not only epidemics kill, but also economic crises which hit the world economy with the force of a Tsunami (Solomon, & Tausch, 2021). Cornia's theses on excess mortality led him to conclude that from 1989 to 2014, 18 million people in the region of Eastern Central Europe and the former USSR fell victim to the gradual economic downturns and shock therapies. The hurricane that is now brewing over the world after the expected health and economic crisis 2020/2021 is already recognizable. The neoliberal set of rules, which determined the West's path after the 2008 financial crisis has caused death rates to climb since 2008 and led to exactly the situation which Cornia describes in his works. Downgraded hospitals in Italy, Spain, the reduction of public services and health services to the limits of state failure, such as in Greece in the wake of the European Stability Mechanism (ESM) austerity packages. Applied to the population as a whole, we must start from the thesis that the 2008 crisis and the subsequent crises in the Eurozone led to the premature death of 1.76

[4] https://www.worldometers.info/coronavirus/.

million people (see Solomon, & Tausch, 2021, reporting calculations, based on https://data.worldbank.org/).[5]

If Russia could have stabilized the death rate at 10.0 per 1000 as in the Brezhnev era, there are 14 million deaths to date that could have been avoided. If the gross death rate had stabilized at 12.0 as at the beginning of perestroika, still 8 million lives could have been saved (our own calculations, based on https://data.worldbank.org/).[6]

But the neoliberal policy framework, which dominated economic policy making won't be easily thrown overboard, and will be prolonging the global economic recession, which now sets in. European elites, especially, are

---

[5] Crude death rates per 1.000 inhabitants in the European Union, according to the World Bank Open Data. available from: https://data.worldbank.org/data, have a clear and straight linear downward trend, which Microsoft EXCEL regression routine (OLS-regression) identifies as being dependent on the time axis with -0,04 as the unstandardized regression coefficient and 86,85 as the constant. Without using more sophisticated models, and predicting crude death rates from this trend after 2008 yields us a first realistic estimate of the crude death rates per 1.000 inhabitants in the European Union, if this good health policy trend would have continued. We compared then these predicted crude death rates per 1.000 inhabitants with the crude death rates after the crisis of 2008, which really exploded, considering the long-term European advances in public health policy before the crisis of 2008. We then projected for each year the numbers of deaths which would have been avoidable, subtracting the crude death rates per 1.000 inhabitants after 2008 from the expected numbers, based on the before-mentioned simple linear regression (regression residuals), which we then weighted with the yearly population figures of the European Union. From 2008 onwards, these figures add up together to 1.76 million human beings who died a death which would have been avoidable had the European Union not experienced the 2008 crisis.

[6] Crude death rates per 1.000 inhabitants in Russia, according to the World Bank Open Data. available from: https://data.worldbank.org/data. We compared Russian crude death rates per 1.000 inhabitants, as they occurred in Russian history, with the crude death rates which were recorded under Brezhnev (variant 1, crude death rate per 1.000 inhabitants = 10.0) and during the onset of "perestroika" (crude death rate per 1.000 inhabitants = 12.0). A simple linear prolongation of public health policy standards during the waning of the communist system would have at least stabilized crude death rates per 1.000 inhabitants enjoyed then in Russia under Brezhnev and enjoyed today by the inhabitants of such countries as Armenia, the Slovak Republic, Slovenia, North Macedonia, and Bosnia and Herzegovina (variant 1) or at last at the beginning of Perestroika then in Russia or in the region of Central Europe and the Baltics (World Bank terminology) today. What happened, however, ever since was not a stabilization of public health, but one of the biggest mortality crises in modern history after the Second World War. Using the mentioned World Bank data, we arrive at the distressing conclusion that up to 12 million people died prematurely (variant 1); or at least 8 million people (lower variant, 2). Simply comparing crude death rates per 1.000 inhabitants in 2017 with those in 2000 reveals another striking aspect: in descending order, Japan, Lithuania, Bosnia and Herzegovina, Romania, Greece, Syrian Arab Republic, Croatia, Albania, Venezuela, RB, North Macedonia, Cuba, Puerto Rico, Armenia, Georgia, Latvia, Mexico, Germany, Serbia, and Poland suffered from an increase in their crude death rates per 1.000 inhabitants over the last 20 years.

currently already hurrying to reactivate the neo-liberal *"rescue umbrella"* (in Chancellor Angela Merkel's language *"Rettungsschirm"*, i.e., the European Stability Mechanism, ESM) that will drive Italy and Spain even more deeply into economic stagnation and into even deeper austerity.

Nobel laureate Hayek laid the foundation for the corset of neoliberal Europe as early as 1939 (Hayek, 1980 (originally 1939); Schulmeister, 2018): In a union of states, (economic) politics had to limit themselves to ensuring that personal initiative can develop optimally in the long term. Hayek explicitly welcomed the downward pressure on wages and social conditions in such a union of states. Unfortunately, what a correct prophecy!

For the present author, it is clear from the data of the IMF, contained in the Global Development Network Growth Database, (https://wp.nyu.edu/dri/resources/global-development-network-growth-database/) and in the IMF World Economic Outlook data base, (https://www.imf.org/external/pubs/ft/weo/2019/02/weodata/index.aspx) that before the great financial crisis in 2008, prolonged budget surpluses were extremely rare in the world economy. Great Britain under PM Margaret Hilda Thatcher is one such rare case (1988 to 1990), and is the only functioning "normal" Western democracy which managed to have a longer budget surplus period without military dictatorship or subsequent state failure, and without enjoying the rare status as an international financial centre (Singapore and Luxembourg) or sizeable oil revenues (Kuwait and Norway). Most instructive for governments both in Europe and the MENA region are the deterrent examples of budget surpluses in Myanmar (under the military rule, 1977-1983); in Chile (under the military dictatorship 1975-76; 1979-1981; 1987-1988) and in communist Romania shortly before the revolution in 1991 (1980-1991). The last example, where long-run budget surpluses were achieved, ex-Yugoslavia, is just as disturbing. Before Yugoslavia collapsed, it achieved a budget surplus in three periods, from 1986 to 1989.[7]

---

[7] https://www.imf.org/en/Data.

But why is the neoliberal budget logic, called the Maastricht criteria, which dominated the entire globe, fundamentally so wrong? In order to understand the policy failures of neoliberalism for much of the 1980s, 1990s and beyond, we have to analyse in more detail how budget policy affects the chances for economic growth. In the European Union, they are responsible for the deep existential crisis of the European South ever since the crisis of 2008, now culminating in the devastation of the health systems in Italy and Spain, and the centrifugal and populist tendencies all across the European continent (Grinin et al., 2016, 2018).

Followers of the economic theory based on Michal Kalecki (1899-1970; Kalecki, 1971), will point out correctly that the private sector of the entire global economy displays a sustained tendency to save more than it invests (see Laski and Podkaminer, 2011, 2012, 2013, 2014). Kazimierz Laski (1921-2015) also pointed out that private investment (IP) minus private saving (SP) plus government deficit (D) and plus net Exports (E) added together always result in zero. So, growth can only be generated by an increase in private investment or by deficit spending or by foreign trade surpluses or by a reduction in the savings rate.

The lessons of the European crisis since 2008 to the MENA countries are also clear by analysing the effects of the European Union's austerity packages (Pollin, 1998; Schulmeister, 2012, 2012, 2014; Stockhammer, 2008; Stockhammer, Constantine and Reissl, 2020):

- The current "integration" of the deficit and debt rule in the EU fiscal pact prescribed to (almost) all EU countries the "Greek way" into depression. The European welfare state was consistently strangled.
- The concept of "natural unemployment" used by the EU Commission forced member states to cut wages and reduce unemployment benefits.

The International Monetary Fund (IMF), in its recent prediction, now expects the global economy to contract by 3 percent in 2020, much worse than during the 2008–09 financial crisis. This scenario still assumes that the pandemic fades in the second half of 2020 and containment efforts can be gradually unwound. The advanced economies will shrink by -6.1%, while China and India still will experience some sort of economic growth by < 2.0%, while the Middle East and North Africa will shrink by around -3.3%. The world will thus be confronted with the largest economic depression since the Great Depression of 1929.

Thanks to the work of Barro and Ursua, 2011, and Barro, Ursua and Weng, 2020, economic science knows much more about the effects of both the Spanish Influenza pandemic from 1918 onwards as well as the Great Depression from 1929 onwards. Since the large literature on long economic cycles, depressions and their devastating effects has been reviewed extensively elsewhere (Grinin et al., 2016), we rather concentrate on analysing what can be expected from the double crisis of a pandemic and a global depression for the countries of the world system in the coming years.

The robust lesson of the "Great Depression" accounting, made possible by the Barro and Ursua, 2011 data is that there are very considerable differences in the way, the Tsunami of the Great Depression hit the countries of the world system in 1929. To recover their pre-depression income level by around + 5%, it took Denmark, Iceland, Korea and Russia only a short lapse of time, and for all practical purposes they recovered already in 1930/31. By 1933/34, Colombia, Greece, Brazil, Finland, Japan, Norway, South Africa, Sweden, and Turkey recovered again.

Only in 1935/36, Italy, Singapore, Taiwan, United Kingdom, Australia, Germany, and New Zealand recovered and had an income level of around +5% above the pre-depression level. In 1937, Portugal and Venezuela followed, while Indonesia only made it in 1938. Even more dramatic, Austria recovered and had an income level of around +5% above the pre-depression level in 1939, the year of the Anschluss, and thus shared the economic misfortunes of Mexico and the Philippines, who also recovered only in 1939. Even worse, Canada and the United States only could recover their income levels in 1940, after the beginning of the Second World War in 1939.

A plus of around 5% or more in the real income levels, compared to 1929, were recorded in the following nations in the following years:

1944: Argentina
1945: Chile
1946: Peru, Switzerland, and Uruguay
1947: Belgium
1949: France
1950: Netherlands
1956: China and Spain
1959: Egypt
After 1960: India, Malaysia and Sri Lanka

There were devastating effects of the Great Depression in China, Spain, the Netherlands, France and Belgium. The economic aftermath of the Great Depression in Peru, Switzerland, Uruguay, Chile, and Argentina was also more than severe:

The world ahead of us is also to be seen, when we correlate the data about relative GDP per capita in PPP (UK, 1913=100) of the countries of the world system, contained in Barro and Ursua, 2011, and Grinin, 2016 with the country death rates of the Great Influenza Epidemic, 1918. The suggestion is that poorer countries were hit harder by the influenza epidemic of 1918 than countries of the centre, although the effect is non-linear due to the higher death rates in some richer countries. The IBM-SPSS 24 calculation of the relationship between the natural logarithm of GDP per capita in the last peace year before the First World War in 1913, UK = 100 and its square and the influenza death rate per country in 1918-20 in the 31 countries is significant at the 1% level, the F ratio is 8.46; the adjusted R^2 is 33.2%, and the predicted infuenza death rate was 13,8860 - 6,1790*ln (GDP per capita PPP, UK, 1913=100) + 0,7160**ln (GDP per capita PPP, UK, 1913=100)^2.

Finally, we risk a prognosis on the overall societal effects of the pandemic. A lesson of the 1918-1920 pandemic is that the severity of the pandemic, as it impacts the different countries of the world, contributes to rising income inequality over time. We measured this by calculating a Pearson correlation of income inequality with the time axis, 1921-1929, based on the Piketty time series data of the share of the richest 1% in total incomes, discussed in Grinin et al., 2016, and the Flu death rates during the Great Influenza Epidemic, 1918-1920 (Barro, Ursua and Weng, 2020). We also attempted to estimate the effects of the severity of the pandemic on international income convergence/divergence over time. To estimate this, we calculated the Pearson correlation of income convergence with the time axis, 1921-1929, based on Maddison data of a country's income per capita in PPP, world average = 100, documented in Grinin et al., 2016, and the severity of the Flu epidemic 1918-1920, measured by the Flu death rates (Barro, Ursua and Weng, 2020). The result is that the severity of an epidemic negatively influences international income convergence over time.

We should finally look at another lesson of history, which might be deduced from the Barro and Ursua, 2011 data. In the UK, it took practically a decade to recover the pre-1918-pandemic income levels, and in Italy, the crisis was even more severe, and Italian democracy collapsed and Benito Mussolini rose to power.

To present a theory or competing theories of 'smart development' is virtually impossible, because there has been no measurement, let alone accounting of its cross-national successes and failures in the literature up to now. We are really had to start research into this issue from 'scratch'.

At a time of a profound global economic crisis, which began in 2008, it might be permitted to look therefore at some of the more radical paradigms, challenging the wisdom of neo-liberal mainstream economic theory. Acemoglu, in his 2009 paper reflecting the lessons of the 2008 crisis, and certainly himself being a leading 'mainstream' and not a 'radical' and 'globalization critical' economist, went on the record of admitting that

> 'There is another sense in which the myth of the end of the business cycle is at odds with fundamental properties of the capitalist system. As Schumpeter argued long ago, the workings of the market system and the innovation dynamics that constitute its essence involve a heavy dose of

> creative destruction, where existing ... firms, procedures and products are replaced by new ones'. (Acemoglu, 2009: 3)

and later on saying:

> 'Economic growth will only take place if the society creates the institutions and policies that encourage innovation, reallocation, investment, and education. But such institutions should not be taken for granted. Because of the reallocation and creative destruction brought about by economic growth, there will always be parties, often strong parties, opposed to certain aspects of economic growth. In many less-developed economies, the key aspect of the political economy of growth is to ensure that incumbent producers, elites and politicians do not hijack the political agenda and create an environment inimical to economic progress and growth. Another threat to the institutional foundations of economic growth comes from its ultimate beneficiaries. Creative destruction and reallocation not only harm established businesses but also their workers and suppliers, sometimes even destroying the livelihood of millions of workers and peasants. It is then easy for impoverished populations suffering from adverse shocks and economic crises, — particularly in societies where the political economy never generated an effective safety net — to turn against the market system and support populist policies that will create barriers against economic growth. These threats are as important for advanced economies as they are for less-developed countries, particularly in the midst of the current economic crisis.' (Acemoglu, 2009: 9-10)

Arguably, the leading flagship article of the economics profession on the issue of the possible general drivers and bottlenecks of economic growth is Levine and Renelt, 1992, which maintains that *empirical linkages* between long-run growth rates and a variety of economic policy, political, and institutional indicators *are fragile to small changes in the conditioning information set.* But there is a positive, robust correlation between growth and the share of investment in GDP and between the investment share and the ratio of international trade to GDP. The variety of relationships, tested in multiple regression analysis, is truly amazing and includes the following non-exhaustive list of variables, which we reproduce here to give our readers, who are not economists, a glimpse of the startling variety of growth predictors, used in economic theory today:

Average inflation of GDP deflator
Black-market exchange-rate premium
Central-government gross capital formation
Dummy for OECD countries
Dummy for OPEC countries
Dummy for outward orientation
Dummy for socialist economy
Dummy sub-Saharan Africa
Dummy variable for Latin American countries
Dummy variable for mixed government
Export share of GDP
Government consumption less defense and education share of GDP
Government consumption share of gross domestic product
Growth of export share of GDP
Growth of exports
Growth of government consumption expenditures
Growth of import share
Growth of imports
Growth of population
Growth of the share of government consumption
Growth rate of domestic credit
Import share of GDP
Index of civil liberties
Investment share of gross domestic product
Land area (in thousands of square kilometers)
Literacy rate in 1960
Measure of openness based on import penetration
Measure of overall trade intervention
Measure of overall trade openness
Number of revolutions and coups per year

Population in 1970
Primary-school enrolment rate in 1960, 1970
Ratio of central-government defense expenditure
Ratio of central-government deficit to GDP
Ratio of central-government export-tax revenue to exports
Ratio of central-government tax revenue to GDP
Ratio of central-government to corporate income-tax revenue to GDP
Ratio of government educational expenditures
Ratio of import taxes to imports
Ratio of social-security tax revenue to GDP
Ratio of total government expenditure to GDP
Ratio of total trade (exports+imports) to GDP
Real exchange-rate distortion
Real government capital formation
Real government consumption share of GDP
Real investment share of GDP
Secondary-school enrolment rate in 1960, 1970
Share of real government consumption expenditures minus defense and education
Standard deviation of GDC (growth of domestic credit)
Standard deviation of PI (inflation)

As the result of their exercise, Levine and Renelt arrive at the following conclusions, which initiated an amazing and unparalleled more than 1.000 follow-up studies in global social science literature to this date:

'(i) We found a positive and robust correlation between average growth rates and the average share of investment in GDP.
(ii) We found a positive and robust correlation between the share of investment in GDP and the average share of trade in GDP.
(iii) We found that all findings using the share of exports in GDP could be obtained almost identically using the total trade or import share. Thus, studies that use export indicators should not be interpreted as studying the relationship between growth and exports per se but rather as

studying the relationship between growth and trade defined more broadly.

(iv) We found that a large variety of trade policy measures were not robustly correlated with growth when the equation included the investment share.

(v) We found qualified support for the conditional-convergence hypothesis: we find a robust, negative correlation between the initial level income and growth over the 1960-1989 period when the equation includes a measure of the initial level of investment in human capital; but this result does not hold over the 1974-1989 period.

(vi) We found that none of the broad array of fiscal indicators that we studied is robustly correlated with growth or the investment share.

(vii) We found that a large assortment of other economic and political indicators are not robustly correlated with growth or the investment share.

We have tried to distinguish partial growth correlations that seem robust from those that are fragile. We find that, although there are many econometric specifications in which macroeconomic policy indicators-taken individually or in groups are significantly correlated with growth, the cross-country statistical relationship between long-run average growth rates and almost every particular macroeconomic indicator is fragile. National policies appear to be a complex package, and future researchers may wish to focus on macroeconomic policy regimes and interactions among policies as opposed to the independent influence of any particular policy.' (Levine and Renelt, 1992: 959-960)

In this presentation of possible theories explaining 'smart development', we now should deal with the notion of *'openness'* or *'world economic openness'*. Globalization critical audiences around the globe might largely disregard the evidence, provided by studies, suggesting that world market integration, not dissociation from the global markets would be the key to long-run economic growth and well-being, but this approach is especially popular in standard economic science, dealing with the issues of international growth accounting over the last decades. The amount and the empirical, i.e., econometric quality of these studies is at first sight overwhelming: *Scopus* listed, by April 22, 2020, 1571 articles on the issue of *'openness'* and *'economic gr*owth', and likewise, the list of scholars, mentioned in Scopus, dealing with this subject, is overwhelming. Some of the world's leading and bestselling economists are among them[8]. Among the studies, listed in international online-bibliographies as especially often being referred to, we find, among others, Alesina, Spolaore and Wacziarg, 2000; Dollar, 1992a and 1992b; Edwards, 1993; Frankel and Romer, 1999; Rodrik, 2006; Rodrik, Subramanian, and Trebbi, 2004; and World Bank, 2005, as well as Furman et al., 2002; Rodríguez and Rodrik, 2000; Bekaert et al., 2005; Sachs and Warner, 1997; and Matsuyama, 1992.

Rodrik, Subramanian, and Trebbi, 2004 shattered the optimistic assumptions about the beneficial effects of world economic openness on development outcomes in their study about the respective contributions of institutions, geography, and trade in determining income levels around the world, using recently developed instrumental variables for institutions and trade. Their results indicate that *'the quality of institutions "trumps" everything else'* (Rodrik, Subramanian, and Trebbi, 2004). Once institutions are controlled for, conventional measures of geography have at best weak direct effects on incomes, although they have a strong indirect effect by influencing the quality of institutions. Similarly, once institutions are controlled for, trade is almost always insignificant, and often enters the income equation with the "wrong" (i.e., negative) sign. In his influential study, 2006, Rodrik even went so far as to fundamentally question the 'Washington Consensus' based on open markets, which featured so prominently in Dollar, 1992a and 1992b:

---

[8] This can be checked easily by looking at the download figures or more complex ranking data, available from the open-access scientific archives like IDEAS/REPEC from the University of Connecticut or the Social Science Research Network, SSRN, in New York, N. Y.

Table 1. Deconstructing the Washington Consensus of liberalization and openness

	Original Washington Consensus		Augmented Washington Consensus
1	Fiscal Discipline	11	Corporate governance
2	Reorientation of public expenditures	12	Anti-corruption
3	Tax reform	13	Flexible labor markets
4	Financial liberalization	14	WTO agreements
5	Unified and competitive exchange rates	15	Financial codes and standards
6	Trade liberalization	16	“Prudent” capital accounting
7	Openness to Direct Foreign Investment	17	Non-intermediate exchange rate regimes
8	Privatization	18	Independent central banks/inflation targeting
9	Deregulation	19	Social safety nets
10	Secure Property Rights	20	Targeted poverty reduction

Source: Rodrik, 2006, based on World Bank, 2005.

The *divisive issue of migration* equally divides opinions around the globe, and it also divides opinions among the global social science research community. Also, it must be mentioned in our theoretical survey. *As it is well-known, migration is part and parcel of the 'four freedoms' of capitalism, besides the freedom of goods, services, and capital.* It is only logical to treat its possible influence on 'smart development' immediately after dealing with the possible effects of 'openness'. *Migration might have a very big effect on 'smart development'.* Migration, after all, assures continued production and hence also pollution in the migration recipient countries, while worker remittances, sent from there to the migration sending countries, might contribute to overall consumption, well-being and investment in environmentally more sustainable housing and heating systems in the migration sending nations (Tausch and Heshmati, 2013): international migration is playing an increasingly important role in developing country economies. As Taylor also pointed out in a number of other studies, especially in 1999, worker remittances are especially affecting the less developed sending countries by the *multiplier effect, well-known in economics since the days of John Maynard Keynes* (Taylor, 2006: 9). *Mass migration* is for Amin (1997) part and parcel of the process of transnational capitalism. Migration is even part of the five pillars of international inequality (Amin, 1997):

a) unequal exchange: the gaps in wages are much greater than the gaps in productivities
b) capital flight from the peripheries to the centres
c) selective migration from the peripheries into the centres
d) the monopoly position of the centres in the international division of labour
e) the control of the centres over the earth's natural resources

In a similar vein, the fellow world system scholar *Immanuel Wallerstein* is implicitly highly critical of the migration optimism of large sectors of the European Left. People migrate, legally or illegally, for obvious reasons. Economic betterment and escape from persecution are the two principal ones. They migrate where they can, and where economic and political prospects for them are best. The recipient areas/countries have always been ambivalent about these migrants. Those in favour of stringent state action against migrants (and not only against illegal migrants) express themselves in xenophobic language, and get support based on a generalized sense of economic and social insecurity in the working and middle classes. This group, in the language of Immanuel Wallerstein, tends to favour building walls and expulsions of various kinds. They usually are located in more conservative political forces but attract support from some groups that normally support parties more on the left. Those opposed to stringent state action are in fact two quite different groups. There are the business elites who welcome migrants in the belief that this enables them to keep wage rates down. And to some extent they are right. They thus want migrants to have the right to enter and to work. But they are not anxious that migrants have political rights, which would enable them to fight for higher remuneration. The second group is quite the opposite. It is composed of the targeted groups plus those on the left who favour increasing, not decreasing, social and political rights for the migrants (Immanuel Wallerstein: http://www.binghamton.edu/fbc/182en.htm).

What are the counter-theories to the dominant neo-liberal development paradigm? For one, the *'Keynesian'* legacy should not be under-estimated. 'Keynesians' would expect *positive trade-offs* to hold between *'government intervention' and the human condition*, and not the other way around. The most consistent counter-perspective to the dominant neo-liberal consensus, often being referred to also as the ,Washington Consensus' is the *Kalecki/Steindl-paradigm.* The Steindl-Kalecki growth policy implications are:

Table 2. The radical counter-perspective of the Kalecki-Steindl-paradigm

Differences in growth strategies	
Steindl–Kaleckian growth policy	Current mainstream on growth
Full employment as main political concerns	Price stability and budget consolidation as main political concerns
Demand as growth driver	Supply as growth driver
Higher effective demand to raise employment	Higher labour market flexibility to raise economic growth
Technology and educational policy	Deregulation and privatization
Lower household savings	Higher savings (for investment)
Stable or rising wage share	Falling wage share (real unit labour costs)
Anticyclical policy (cycle and trend have the same determinants)	No active anticyclical policy (irrelevant for growth path)
Rise of public sector promotes growth (through effective demand)	Decline and restructuring of the public sector (efficiency)
Tax coordination	International tax competition
International cooperation	International competition (location)

Source: Guger/Marterbauer/Walterskirchen, 2004 and Tausch and Heshmati, 2013.

The contribution of the Austrian political economist Josef Steindl (1912--1993), whose work nowadays enjoys a renaissance (see also: Lavoie, 1996) is perceived by many as the most consistent policy alternative to the current, dominant Brussels/Paris neo-liberal consensus of the European Commission and the OECD. In Steindl (1946), the author analyzed the process of increasing concentration of capital and the oligopoly of the market. The change in the secular trend of income distribution since the end of the Second World War in the world's most advanced economies, observed by Steindl, has to be especially noted: since the early 1980s, income distribution has changed in favour of classes with high savings propensities; i.e., in most industrial countries the share of wages and salaries in national income has been declining, while non-wage income, in particular property income, has risen sharply, and income inequality between the rich and the poor has increased considerably.

According to Steindl, the burden of taxation has shifted from profits to wages - a process which reduced the expansionary effects of the public sector (Steindl, 1979, p. 5). Assuming that tax revenues are immediately spent, higher profit taxes are paid out of increasing profits (before taxation) due to higher capital utilization, while an increase in wage taxation reduces consumption. The following aspects of Steindl's analysis especially caught the attention of the empirical researchers from the Austrian Institute of Economic Research (Guger/Marterbauer/Walterskirchen, 2006): what Steindl calls a *'policy of stagnation'* will continue, since governments are preoccupied with inflation and the public debt (Steindl, 1979, p. 9). Thus the Steindl paper on *'Stagnation Theory and Stagnation Policy'* (Steindl, 1979, especially p. 13) must be regarded, as one of the first key documents against the current Euro-monetarist stagnation policy, which – according to this Kaleckian viewpoint – is the cause of stagnation, unemployment and rising inequality in Europe. The new political and economic landscape, which began to take shape in the late 1970s and 1980s, was characterized by:

- macroeconomic policy being oriented primarily towards price stability and budget consolidation
- declining international cooperation regarding economic policy (breakdown of the Bretton Woods system and the establishment of a flexible exchange rate system in the early 1970s)
- increasing environmental and energy problems
- a political trend against full employment (with Kalecki, 1943). Steindl believed in the 'political aspects of full employment'. This hypothesis, first published by Kalecki in 1943, argued that in the long run the entrepreneurs will be losing interest in full employment because of the increasing power of trade unions and employees as a consequence of full employment. As predicted by Kalecki in 1943,

the end of the period of full employment, which came about in the late 1960s, was politically motivated.

This new set-up was called by Steindl the *'return of the Bourbons'*. In terms of thoroughly tested scientific knowledge, based on large-scale, cross-national empirical evidence, the next possible alternative theoretical tradition to fill the explanatory gap for 'smart development' accounting, coming to one's mind, would be *dependency and world systems theory*. Although its effect on the mainstream economic scholarly journals has been marginal, it had a very wide impact on the leading international sociological and political journals[9].

Reasons of space do not permit us to debate at greater length this very vast sociological, political science and economic theory literature, centred on the subject of MNC (multinational corporation) penetration and economic and social development. We refer interested readers to more recent summaries of this vast debate, including Tausch and Heshmati, 2013.

There was a real 'growth industry' of blossoming and booming dependency - and world-system oriented studies of environmental problems during the last years. It has become really fashionable in many traditions of sociology and political science to blame the lack of *'sustainable development'* on globalization and the workings of global capitalism, perceived as a centre-periphery system.

---

[9] International quantitative bibliometrical data on the impact of scholarly journals, i.e. the frequency and structure of the references in the international literature, are now available from such indices as SCIMAGO (http://www.scimagojr.com/, based on SCIVERSE-SCOPUS), ISI Web of Knowledge (Reuters/Thomson http://www.isiwebofknowledge.com/) and SCIVERSE-SCOPUS (Elsevier http://www.hub.sciverse.com/action/home/proceed), which are available on-line at major Universities and research centres around the globe.

Table 3. The major globalization critical studies about dependency and the environment

Author	Year	Title	Source	Research design focused on	Anti-globalization approach
Dick, Ch. and Jorgenson, A. K.	2010	Sectoral Foreign Investment and Nitrous Oxide Emissions: A Quantitative Investigation	Society and Natural Resources, vol. 23(1), 71-82, 2010	nitrous oxide emissions	Confirmed
Ehrhardt-Martinez, Karen; Crenshaw, Edward M.; Jenkins, J. Craig	2002	Deforestation and the Environmental Kuznets Curve: A Cross-National Investigation of Intervening Mechanisms	Social Science Quarterly, vol. 83(1), 226-243, Mar 2002	deforestation	Rejected
Jorgenson, A. K.	2003	Consumption and environmental degradation: A cross-national analysis of the ecological footprint	Social Probems, 50, 3, 374-394	ecological footprint	Confirmed
Jorgenson, A. K.	2007	Does foreign investment harm the air we breathe and the water we drink? A cross-national study of carbon dioxide emissions and organic water pollution in less-developed countries, 1975 to 2000	Organization & Environment, 20, 2, 135-157, 2007	carbon dioxide emissions; emission of organic water pollutants	Confirmed
Jorgenson, A. K.	2006	Unequal ecological exchange and environmental degradation: A theoretical proposition and cross-national study of deforestation, 1990-2000	Rural Sociology, 71, 4, 685-712, 2006	deforestation	Confirmed
Jorgenson, A. K. and Burns, T. J.	2007	The political-economic causes of change in the ecological footprints of nations, 1991-2001: A quantitative investigation	Social Science Research, 36, 2, 834-853	growth of ecological footprint	Confirmed
Jorgenson, A. K., Dick, C., and Mahutga, M. C.	2007	Foreign investment dependence and the environment: An ecostructural approach	Social Problems, 54, 3, 371-394	nitrogen oxides, volatile organic compounds, carbon monoxide, and carbon dioxide gas	Confirmed

Table 3. (Continued).

Author	Year	Title	Source	Research design focused on	Anti-globalization approach
Jorgenson, Andrew K	2008	Structural Integration and the Trees: An Analysis of Deforestation in Less-Developed Countries, 1990-2005	The Sociological Quarterly, vol. 49(3), 503-527, Summer 2008	deforestation	Confirmed
Jorgenson, Andrew K.	2004	Uneven Processes and Environmental Degradation in the World-Economy	Human Ecology Review, vol. 11(2), 103-117, summer 2004	ecological footprint	Confirmed
Jorgenson, Andrew K.	2005	Unpacking International Power and the Ecological Footprints of Nations: A Quantitative Cross-National Study	Sociological Perspectives, vol. 48(3), 383-402, fall 2005	ecological footprint	Confirmed
Jorgenson, Andrew K.	2006	Global Warming and the Neglected Greenhouse Gas: A Cross-National Study of the Social Causes of Methane Emissions Intensity, 1995	Social Forces, vol. 84(3), 1779-1798, Mar 2006	greenhouse gas emissions	Confirmed
Jorgenson, Andrew K.	2009	Political-Economic Integration, Industrial Pollution and Human Health: A Panel Study of Less-Developed Countries, 1980--2000	International Sociology, vol. 24(1), 115-143, Jan 2009	industrial organic water pollution, infant mortality	Confirmed
Jorgenson, Andrew K.	2007	Foreign Direct Investment and Pesticide Use Intensity in Less-Developed Countries: A Quantitative Investigation	Society and Natural Resources, vol. 20(1), 73-83, Jan 2007	pesticide consumption	Confirmed
Jorgenson, Andrew K.	2009	The Transnational Organization of Production, the Scale of Degradation, and Ecoefficiency: A Study of Carbon Dioxide Emissions in Less-Developed Countries	Human Ecology Review, vol. 16(1), 64-74, Summer 2009	total carbon dioxide emissions and emissions per unit of production	Confirmed
Jorgenson, Andrew K.	2004	Global Inequality, Water Pollution, and Infant Mortality	The Social Science Journal, vol. 41(2), 279-288, 2004	water pollution, infant mortality	Confirmed
Jorgenson, Andrew K.; Burns, Thomas J.	2004	Globalization, the Environment, and Infant Mortality: A Cross National Study	Humboldt Journal of Social Relations, vol. 28(1), 7-52, 2004	water pollution, infant mortality	Confirmed

Author	Year	Title	Source	Research design focused on	Anti-globalization approach
Jorgenson, Andrew K.; Kuykendall, Kennon A.	2008	Globalization, Foreign Investment Dependence and Agriculture Production: Pesticide and Fertilizer Use in Less-developed Countries, 1990-2000	Social Forces, vol. 87(1), 529-560, Sept 2008	pesticide and fertilizer use	Confirmed
Lawrence, Kirk S	2009	The Thermodynamics of Unequal Exchange	International Journal of Comparative Sociology, vol. 50(3)-4, 335-359, June/Aug 2009	energy use	Confirmed
Longo, Stefano; York, Richard	2008	Agricultural Exports and the Environment: A Cross-National Study of Fertilizer and Pesticide Consumption	Rural Sociology, vol. 73(1), 82-104, Mar. 2008	fertilizer and pesticide consumption	Confirmed
Mostafa, M. M.	2010	A Bayesian approach to analyzing the ecological footprint of 140 nations	Ecological Indicators, 10, 4, 808-817, 2010	ecological footprint	Confirmed
Mostafa, M. M.	2010	Clustering the ecological footprint of nations using Kohonen's self-organizing maps	Expert Systems with Applications, 37, 4, 2747-2755	ecological footprint per capita	Confirmed
Mostafa, M. M. and Nataraajan, R.	2009	A neuro-computational intelligence analysis of the ecological footprint of nations	Computational Statistics and Data Analysis, 53, 9, 3516-3531, 2009	ecological footprint	Confirmed
Nugent, Colleen and Shandra, John M.	2009	State Environmental Protection Efforts, Women's Status, and World Polity A Cross-National Analysis	Organization & Environment, 22, 3, 293-310, 2009	environmental protection efforts	Confirmed
Shandra, J. M., Leckband, C., McKinney, L. A, and London, B.	2009	Ecologically Unequal Exchange, World Polity, and Biodiversity Loss A Cross-National Analysis of Threatened Mammals	International Journal of Comparative Sociology, 50, 3-4, 285-310, 2009	threatened mammal species	Confirmed
Shandra, John M.	2007	Economic dependency, repression, and deforestation: A quantitative, cross-national analysis	Sociological Inquiry, 77, 4, 543-571, 2007	deforestation	Confirmed
Shandra, John M.	2007	International nongovernmental organizations and deforestation: Good, bad, or irrelevant?	Social Science Quarterly, 88, 3, 665-689, 2007	deforestation	Confirmed

Table 3. (Continued).

Author	Year	Title	Source	Research design focused on	Anti-globalization approach
Shandra, John M. Leckband, Christopher London, Bruce	2009	Ecologically Unequal Exchange and Deforestation: A Cross-National Analysis of Forestry Export Flows	Organization & Environment, 22, 2, 208-229, 2009	deforestation	Confirmed
Shandra, John M. Shandra, Carrie L. London, Bruce	2008	Women, non-governmental organizations, and deforestation: a cross-national study	Population and Environment, 30, 1-2, 48-72, 2008	deforestation	Confirmed
Shandra, John M. Shor, Eran London, Bruce	2009	World Polity, Unequal Ecological Exchange, and Organic Water Pollution: A Cross-National Analysis of Developing Nations	Human Ecology Review, 16, 1, 53-63, 2009	organic water pollution	Confirmed
Shandra, John M.; London, Bruce; Whooley, Owen P.; Williamson, John B.	2004	International Nongovernmental Organizations and Carbon Dioxide Emissions in the Developing World: A Quantitative, Cross-National Analysis	Sociological Inquiry, vol. 74(4), 520-545, Nov 2004	carbon dioxide emissions	Confirmed
Shandra, John M; Shor, Eran; London, Bruce	2008	Debt, Structural Adjustment, and Organic Water Pollution	Organization & Environment, vol. 21(1), 38-55, Mar. 2008	organic water pollution	Confirmed
Tausch, Arno	2007	Quantitative World System Studies Contradict Current Islamophobia: World Political Cycles, Global Terrorism, and World Development	Alternatives: Turkish Journal of International Relations, vol. 6(1)-2, 15-81, spring-summer 2007	11 indicators of development, including environmental indicators	Confirmed
Tausch, Arno	2005	Is Islam really a development blockade?	Insight Turkey, vol. 7(1), 124-135, Jan-Mar 2005	14 indicators of development, including environmental indicators	Confirmed
Tausch, Arno	2003	Social Cohesion, Sustainable Development and Turkey's Accession to the European Union: Implications from a Global Model	Alternatives. Turkish Journal of International Relations, Vol. 2(1), 2003	14 indicators of development, including environmental indicators	Confirmed

Table 3 presents the main literature trends. Only one of the 34 studies in the major peer-reviewed journals of international social science surveyed contradicted the globalization critical approach. It has to be emphasized, however, that these studies relate the environmental situation of a given country to achieved development levels, without taking into account the relationship between development results and the natural resources needed to sustain them. The central question, posed by Meadows, 1992, and by the Happy Planet Index methodology is not how much deforestation, ecological destruction etc. we face in the world system at given levels of development, but how much footprint was consumed in the nations of the world system to 'deliver' a given amount of development [democracy, economic growth, gender equality, human development, research and development, and social cohesion].

Notably enough, only three of these 34 studies (Tausch, 2003, 2005, 2007) used the combined Yale/Columbia indices of the environmental situation, the 'Environmental Sustainability Index (ESI)' and the 'Environmental Performance Index (EPI)', already available since the middle of the first decade of the third Millennium for a very wide range of countries.

It is now time to present also some thoughts on the other control variables. A number of high-profile studies in economics have used such control variables, while the sociological profession seems to be more cautious about their use[10]. For reasons of space, we refer interested readers to Table 4 of this study.

Finally, we should mention here the works of the economists *Ernst Friedrich 'Fritz' Schumacher* (16 August 1911 – 4 September 1977) and *Leopold Kohr* (5 October 1909 – 26 February 1994.[11] Their work is often being referred to today as *'Buddhist economics'*. We already drew our reader's attention to the fact that on an international level, the Happy Planet Organization indicators[12] – Ecological Footprint, Happy Life Years, and the

---

[10] Interested readers are also referred to Easterly, 2000, 2002; Easterly and Levine, 1997; Heshmati and Tausch, 2007 for further reference.

[11] The most important ideas by Kohr and Schumacher were stated in Kohr, 1957, 1958, 1960, 1977, 1992 and Schumacher, 1973a, 1973b, 1976, 1977.

[12] http://www.happyplanetindex.org/.

derived measure Happy Planet Index (HPI), which measures the ecological efficiency with which human well-being is delivered around the world, increasingly gained in importance. At first sight, the measure is of a compelling simplicity, capturing at the same time the growing global ecological concerns about the validity of our lifestyle, needing more and more energy to produce a stagnant or even shrinking rate of human happiness. Accordingly, the basic logic of the Happy Planet Index must be traced back especially to Schumacher's writings.[13] Schumacher's *'Buddhist economics'* are based on an envisaged minimum material consumption in relation to life quality. Internationally, we observe a growing framework of what is being increasingly referred-to as *'the environmental efficiency of well-being'* (EWEB, see also Dietz, Rosa and York, 2007 and 2009; Knight and Rosa, 2011). Schumacher's critique of Western economies and his proposals for human-scale, decentralized and appropriate technologies led him to call for 'Intermediate Size' and 'Intermediate Technology'.[14] Schumacher, in many ways, must be considered as one of the founders of contemporary thinking about *'sustainable development'*. Central for Schumacher's concerns is the idea that in rich countries these developments can be partly compensated, as far as incomes are concerned, by an enormous and never ending expansion of welfare payments; in poor countries it produces 'dual societies' - great masses of destitute people on the one side - many of them without work and living in slums - and a small, rich elite on the other, who often 'earn' in an hour more than most of their compatriots earn in a month. A genuine middle class to connect the extremes does not exist; it has disappeared together with the 'disappearing middle' of technology. The loss of social structure is paralleled by the loss of a coherent structure as far as human settlements are concerned: hence the appearance of vast congestion in a few places and a vast (relative) emptiness in all other places. (Schumacher, 1973b; 1976). Schumacher's alternative strategy is based on the factors of smallness, simplicity, capital-cheapness and non-violence. Schumacher was also among the first to highlight the enormous

---

[13] see http://www.resurgence.org/education/schumacher-circle.html#ne.

[14] For a very good overview of Schumacherian economics, see also http://www.resurgence.org/education/schumacher-circle.html#ne.

dependence of modern, industrialized agriculture on fossil fuels. Harvested crops capture solar energy and store it as food or some other useful product. Yet the energy captured is small compared to the energy we burn to capture it. Agriculture, as a result, has become a major consumer of our stores of energy, using more petroleum than any other single industry. If the world is facing a future with rising energy prices, the highly mechanized technology currently used in modern, industrialized agriculture may be inappropriate (Schumacher, 1973b).

In Schumacher, 1973b, it is already being argued that government effort must be concentrated on sustainable development, because relatively minor improvements, for example, technology transfer to Third World countries, will not solve the underlying problem of an unsustainable economy. Schumacher indeed was one of the first economists to question the appropriateness of gross national product as a measure for human well being, emphasizing that 'the aim ought to be to obtain the maximum amount of well being with the minimum amount of consumption' (Schumacher, 1973b).

For Kohr's approach, the consequences are even more radical:[15] there seems only one cause behind all forms of social misery: bigness. Whenever something is wrong, something is too big. Social problems have the tendency to grow at a geometric ratio with the growth of the organism of which they are part, while the ability of man to cope with them, if it can be extended at all, grows only at an arithmetic ratio. For Kohr it is clear that if a society grows beyond its optimum size, its problems must eventually outrun the growth of those human faculties which are necessary for dealing with them. A small-state world would not only solve the problems of social brutality and war; it would solve the problems of oppression and tyranny. It would solve all problems arising from power (Kohr, 1957):

> 'As regards the scale of socially committed or condoned atrocities, we have so far discovered one fact. Most nations, irrespective of their racial background, the stage of their civilization, their ideology, or their economic system, have managed to roll up an impressively similar record.

---

[15] Kohr, 1957, 1958, 1960, 1977, 1992.

> Mass executions and related monstrosities were perpetrated in Germany under the nazis, in India under the British, in France under the Catholics, in Russia under some of the most savage, and in Italy under some of the most enlightened, princes. There could not have been a vaster difference of conditions. Yet, if similar excesses occurred everywhere and in all phases and periods of historic development, there must apparently be a common element transcending these differences. This common denominator, as we shall see, seems to be the simple ability, the power, to commit monstrosities. As a result, we arrive at what we might call a power theory of social misery. In part, the proposition seems self-evident. For no one could perpetrate atrocities without the power to do so. But this is not the point. The point is that the proposition operates also in the reverse. Everyone having the power will in the end commit the appropriate atrocities. This sounds somewhat extreme. Clearly, not everybody holding power must necessarily make evil use of it. Which is quite true, but it does not alter the proposition'. (Kohr, 1957, Chapter II)

Confronted with all this startling variety of contradictory statements on the drivers and bottlenecks of international development, we now should present a survey of the empirical methods used in this study.

Chapter 2

METHODS AND MEASUREMENT

This book was written in the tradition of macro-quantitative development research. We especially mention what can be termed “development accounting” (see: Grinin et al., 2016; Tausch 2010; Tausch, & Heshmati, 2012, 2013). We also portray our research results at the level of choropleth maps.[16]

Our macro-comparative methodology is also oriented by recent advances in this field (see: Babones, 2014; Holland, & Campbell, 2005; Tausch, Heshmati, & Karoui, 2014). We also apply advanced econometric time series techniques, like spectral analysis and analyses of autocorrelations, to the MENA country data (as to the description of these techniques, see Grinin, Korotayev, & Tausch, 2016).

General datasets, used in the present analysis, were:

- *Global Development Network Growth Database,* https://wp.nyu.edu/dri/resources/global-development-network-growth-database/ based on IMF
- *IMF World Economic Outlook* data base, freely available from https://www.imf.org/external/pubs/ft/weo/2019/02/weodata/index.aspx

---

[16] The choropleth maps of this chapter were drawn using the free software developed by Robert Mundigl, available at https://www.clearlyandsimply.com/.

- *KOF Globalisation Index.* Data definitions and free download available from: https://kof.ethz.ch/prognosen-indikatoren/indikatoren/kof-globalisierungsindex.html.[17]
- *UNDP Human Development Data.* Data definitions and free download available from: http://hdr.undp.org/en/data.
- *UTIP Inequality Index.* Data definitions and free download available from: https://utip.lbj.utexas.edu/data.html
- *World Bank Open Data.* Data definitions and free download available from: https://data.worldbank.org/.

In addition, special emphasis was given to dependency and world system approaches to development, which received a large-scale empirical confirmation in Tausch, & Heshmati, 2013 (see also Bornschier, 1980, 1983, Bornschier, & Ballmer-Cao, 1979; Bornschier, & Chase-Dunn, 1985; Tausch, 2010, 2012, Tausch, & Heshmati, 2012). Datasets for these investigations were

- Bornschier, & Ballmer-Cao, 1978
- Müller, & Bornschier, 1988
- Tausch, 2012 [*International Macroquantitative Data.* Faculty of Economics, Corvinus University of Budapest (with data definitions and sources). Free download available from http://www.uni-corvinus.hu/index.php?id=47854&tx_ttnews%5Btt_news%5D=0&tx_ttnews%5BbackPid%5D=31638&tx_ttnews%5BcalendarYear%5D=2012&tx_ttnews%5BcalendarMonth%5D=6&cHash=af8ef6888f7c9922b83b113f71c1ca32]

More recent databases, integrating dependency and world system approaches with conventional economic theories and the sociology of world values research are:

[17] Data definitions for the current version of the KOF Index are available from: https://ethz.ch/content/dam/ethz/special-interest/dual/kof-dam/documents/Globalization/2018/Definitions_2018_2.pdf.

- Tausch, 2019. [*Migration from the Muslim world to the West: Its most recent trends and effects.* Jewish Political Studies Review, 30(1-2), 65-225, available at http://jcpa.org/article/migration-from-the-muslim-world-to-the-west-its-most-recent-trends-and-effects/ (with data definitions and sources). Free data download available from https://www.academia.edu/37568941/Migration_from_the_Muslim_World_to_the_West_Its_Most_Recent_Trends_and_Effects]
- Tausch & Heshmati, 2013 [*Globalisation, the human condition, and sustainable development in the twenty-first century: cross-national perspectives and European implications.* London, New York and Delhi: Anthem Press (with data definitions and sources). Free data download available from https://www.academia.edu/35044095/Globalization_the_human_condition_and_sustainable_development_in_the_21st_Century._Cross-national_perspectives_and_European_implications_Codebook_and_EXCEL_data_file]

Our statistical calculations were performed by the routine and standard SPSS statistical program (SPSS XXIV),[18] available at many academic research centres around the world and relied on the so-called oblique rotation of the factors, underlying the correlation matrix (Tausch, Heshmati and Karoui, 2014).[19] The SPSS routine chosen in this context was the so-called *promax* rotation of factors (Tausch, Heshmati and Karoui, 2014), which in many ways must be considered to be the best suited rotation of factors in the context of our research.[20] Since both our data and the statistical methods used are available around the globe, any researcher can repeat our research exercise with the available open data and should be able to reproduce the

---

[18] https://www-01.ibm.com/software/at/analytics/spss/.

[19] https://www.ibm.com/analytics/spss-statistics-software. The authors express thanks to the Department of Political Science, Innsbruck University, https://www.uibk.ac.at/politikwissenschaft/index.html.en for the opportunity to be able to use the software.

[20] Older approaches often assumed that there is no correlation between the factors, best representing the underlying dimensions of the variables. But for example, in attempting to understand the recent pro-Brexit vote in the United Kingdom it would be ridiculous to assume that, say, there is no correlation between anti-immigration attitudes and anti-European Union attitudes.

same results as we did. Literature searches were carried out with the *Scopus* data base.[21]

Our investigation duly acknowledges many of the key determinants of economic growth, mentioned in the economic literature, like current shares of the country's inhabitants in total world population, calculated from UNDP data; the famous Heritage Foundation 2000 Economic Freedom Score; absolute geographical latitude, adapted from Easterly's growth theory; the UNDP figures for long-term annual population growth rate, 1975-2005 (per cent); the trade-off between development level and development performance, otherwise also known in economics as 'conditional convergence' (ln GDP per capita; ln GDP per capita ^2); the simple Huntingtonian fact of whether a country is a Muslim country, to be measured by the Organization of Islamic Conference (OIC) Membership or by Muslim population share (Nationmaster); UNDP data on the simple geographical fact of population density (based on the CIA's World Factbook); UNDP data on public education expenditure per GDP; and the UNDP education index, combining the enrolment rates at the primary, secondary and tertiary education levels. We also take into account UNDP figures on military expenditures per GDP and the openly available CIA data on military personnel rate, which are key variables of contemporary political science international relations theory and peace research. In our analysis, we also show the theoretical and practical (political) potential of the following two drivers of development, which are somewhat a 'terra incognita Australis' in the hitherto existing macro-sociological debate, like migration and European (Monetary) Union membership.

To gain a real empirical knowledge under scrutiny here, we first developed UNDP-type indicators from current standard international comparative, cross-national social science data on these six dimensions of development and on the combined performance on the six dimensions. We then show the non-linear standard OLS regression trade-off between ecological footprint per capita and its square and these six dimensions of

[21] https://www.scopus.com/home.uri. The authors express thanks to the Department of Development Studies, Vienna University, https://ie.univie.ac.at/en/ for the opportunity to be able to use Scopus.

development (and the overall development performance indices). The residuals from these regressions are our new measure of smart development: with a minimum of ecological footprint one has to achieve a maximum of democracy, or economic growth, or gender equality, or human development, or research and development, or social cohesion (and the combination of all of them). We then look in a very preliminary way at the drivers and bottlenecks of smart development. Can the accumulated knowledge of cross-national development research be applied to this new question writing? We use standard comparative cross-national 'development accounting' data, which operationalize standard econometric drivers of economic growth, and compare their weight in explaining 'smart development' with the results for the clash of civilization models, political integration theories, feminist theories, migration theories, and peace research approaches to global development. We also analyze the possible explanatory weight of sociological dependency and world systems theories and later globalization critical research, and also do not overlook in our choice of independent variables with a possible effect on the dependent variables – smart development - the *'small is beautiful paradigm'* in the tradition of Schumacher.

Instead of concentrating on the ever more complex modelling of the effects of *'foreign capital dependence',* the economics profession, by contrast, developed its mathematical models of 'development accounting' side by side with an ever-growing amount of many different variables, which featured as *'control variables'* in the literature. An attempt, like the one by Sala-i-Martin (1997), to filter out the most robust predictors of economic growth by applying Bayesian techniques and combining dozens of predictor variables in all mathematically possible different combinations is a very legitimate one from the viewpoint of the advancement of social science and statistical methodology. By contrast, sociologists used to the published articles in journals like the *'American Sociological Review'* most probably would be shocked by Sala-i-Martin's successful attempt to run *two million regressions* (in a scientific paper version of his 1997 essay, he even speaks about *four million regressions*). Availability of computer power, common databases and search engines with same on-line journal service may finally bring the three disciplines of sociology, politics and economics closer.

The question of the geographic, demographic and other independent variables in development accounting found much more attention in the recent *economic* literature. According to this type of research, we currently are facing around 100 popular independent variables in the current econometric literature on the determinants of economic growth. Sala-i-Martin, Doppelhofer and Miller, 2004, arrived at the following list of robust growth predictors, which keep their significance after all possible relevant changes in the research design, applying their Bayesian estimation techniques:

1. East Asian dummy
2. Primary schooling 1960
3. Investment price
4. GDP 1960 (log)
5. Fraction tropical area
6. Population density coastal 1960's
7. Malaria prevalence in 1960's
8. Life expectancy in 1960
9. Fraction Confucian
10. African dummy
11. Latin American dummy
12. Fraction GDP in mining
13. Spanish colony
14. Years open
15. Fraction Muslim
16. Fraction Buddhist
17. Ethno-linguistic fractionalization
18. Government consumption share 1960s

The choice of a country to be included in the final analysis (175 countries[22]) was determined by the availability of a fairly good data series for these independent variables (if not mentioned otherwise, UNDP data for the middle of the first decade of the new millennium). In the final regressions, we applied the 'list wise deletion of missing values' routine (i.e. only entering countries with complete data into the statistical analysis).

For the interested readers, Box 1 summarizes this 'dependency theory'/'world systems theory' 'empirical logic':

Box 1. The logic of dependency and the capitalist world system, challenging neo-liberal orthodoxies

MNC penetration (MNC PEN) measures the different degrees of weight that foreign capital investments have in the host countries, i.e., the UNCTAD percentages of the stocks of multinational corporation investments per total host country GDP. This research tradition has been especially developed, as mentioned earlier, by the Swiss sociologist Volker Bornschier and his school. Bornschier and his school predicted a strong negative determination of development by a high MNC penetration, due to the negative consequences that monopolies have on the long term development trajectory of countries.

- We also ascertain the **growth of MNC penetration over time (DYN MNC PEN)**, from 1995 to 2005. The Bornschier School expected short-term dynamic effects from such MNC penetration increases.

---

[22] Albania; Algeria; Angola; Antigua and Barbuda; Argentina; Armenia; Australia; Austria; Azerbaijan; Bahamas; Bahrain; Bangladesh; Barbados; Belarus; Belgium; Belize; Benin; Bhutan; Bolivia; Bosnia and Herzegovina; Botswana; Brazil; Brunei Darussalam; Bulgaria; Burkina Faso; Burundi; Cambodia; Cameroon; Canada; Cape Verde; Central African Republic; Chad; Chile; China; Colombia; Comoros; Congo; Congo (Democratic Republic of the); Costa Rica; Côte d'Ivoire; Croatia; Cuba; Cyprus; Czech Republic; Denmark; Djibouti; Dominica; Dominican Republic; Ecuador; Egypt; El Salvador; Equatorial Guinea; Eritrea; Estonia; Ethiopia; Fiji; Finland; France; Gabon; Gambia; Georgia; Germany; Ghana; Greece; Grenada; Guatemala; Guinea; Guinea-Bissau; Guyana; Haiti; Honduras; Hong Kong, China (SAR); Hungary; Iceland; India; Indonesia; Iran (Islamic Republic of); Ireland; Israel; Italy; Jamaica; Japan; Jordan; Kazakhstan; Kenya; Korea (Republic of); Kuwait; Kyrgyzstan; Lao People's Democratic Republic; Latvia; Lebanon; Lesotho; Libyan Arab Jamahiriya; Lithuania; Luxembourg; Macedonia (TFYR); Madagascar; Malawi; Malaysia; Maldives; Mali; Malta; Mauritania; Mauritius; Mexico; Moldova; Mongolia; Morocco; Mozambique; Myanmar; Namibia; Nepal; Netherlands; New Zealand; Nicaragua; Niger; Nigeria; Norway; Oman; Pakistan; Panama; Papua New Guinea; Paraguay; Peru; Philippines; Poland; Portugal; Qatar; Romania; Russian Federation; Rwanda; Saint Kitts and Nevis; Saint Lucia; Saint Vincent and the Grenadines; Samoa; Sao Tome and Principe; Saudi Arabia; Senegal; Seychelles; Sierra Leone; Singapore; Slovakia; Slovenia; Solomon Islands; South Africa; Spain; Sri Lanka; Sudan; Suriname; Swaziland; Sweden; Switzerland; Syrian Arab Republic; Tajikistan; Tanzania (United Republic of); Thailand; Timor-Leste; Togo; Trinidad and Tobago; Tunisia; Turkey; Turkmenistan; Uganda; Ukraine; United Arab Emirates; United Kingdom; United States; Uruguay; Uzbekistan; Vanuatu; Venezuela (Bolivarian Republic of); Vietnam; Yemen; Zambia; and Zimbabwe.

- Equally, Bornschier and his school already developed a high theoretical and empirical awareness about the long-term consequences of the presence or absence of **'MNC headquarter status' (MNC HEADQU),** measured in our analysis by the indicator MNC outward investments (stock) per GDP. Bornschier and his school expected that a high headquarter status mitigates against the long-term negative effects of MNC penetration.
- **FPZ (free production zones)** employment as a per cent of total population is the indicator best suited to measure the so-called 'NIDL' (new international division of labour) school. Early on, Froebel, Heinrichs and Kreye (1980) already predicted the unfettered rise of the model of 'export processing zones', especially in China and Southeast Asia. This first major international study by Froebel/Heinrichs/Kreye, 1980 was followed, among others, by Ross, 2004; and Singa-Boyenge, 2007. Export Processing Zones (EPZ) – or ***'Free Production Zones'*** today already account for some 80 per cent of the merchandise exports of countries like China, Kenya, the Philippines, Malaysia, Mauritius, Mexico, Senegal, Tunisia, and Vietnam. The 3500 EPZs in 130 countries of the world now employ 66 million people, among these 40 million employees in China. The tendency, correctly foreseen by Froebel/Heinrichs/Kreye, 1980 towards this total global re-location of world industries continues unabated. In the present book, we try to determine the quantitative weights, which free production zones have in the determination of development performance (per cent of the population working in export processing zones versus MNC penetration versus the other dependency/globalization indicators).
- **'low comparative price levels'** (for an exhaustive debate on the underlying issues from a dependency theory/world systems perspective, see Kohler/Tausch, 2003, furthermore Raffer, 1987, Yotopoulos, 1996, and Yotopoulos/Sawada, 2005 from a dependency theory/world systems perspective, as well as Balassa, 1964 and Samuelson, 1964 from a more conventional economic theory framework) is operationalized here simply by ERD or ERDI, the exchange rate deviation index, which is calculated by the ratio between GDP at purchasing power parities, divided by GDP at current exchange rates (see also http://epp.eurostat.ec.europa.eu/portal/page/portal/structural_indicators/indicators/economic_reform). Dependency theories and world systems theories assume that low comparative price levels are an indicator of 'unequal exchange' between the countries of the center and the periphery.[23]
- For dependency authors, **foreign savings** show the weight that foreign savings, mostly from the centres and richer semi-peripheries, have in the accumulation process of the host countries in the periphery and semi-periphery. It is calculated by the difference between the share of investments per GDP and the share of savings per GDP.

Table 4. The independent variables of our model and theories or earlier empirical studies, connected with these variables

Independent variables, determinants of smart development	Theories or earlier empirical studies, connected with these variables
% women in government, all levels	Holmberg, Rothstein and Nasiritousi, 2009; Logo, 2008; Matt, 2010; McDowell, 1992; Orloff, 1996; Rankin, 2002; Rothstein and Teorell; UNDP, HDR, 1995
% world population	Acemoglu and Dell, 2010; Acemoglu and Robinson, 2000, 2001, 2006; Acemoglu, 2003, 2005, 2010a, 2010b; Acemoglu, Johnson and

[23] For an easily readable and available survey of the available and often very complicated literature as well as the empirics of 'unequal exchange', see Kohler/Tausch, 2003 and http://wsarch.ucr.edu/archive/papers/kohlertoc.htm.

Independent variables, determinants of smart development	Theories or earlier empirical studies, connected with these variables
	Robinson, 2001, 2002, 2005; Amin, 1997a, 1997b; Crenshaw and Robison, 2010; Kohr, 1957, 1958, 1960, 1977, 1992; Ram, 1997; Schumacher, 1973a, 1973b, 1976, 1977
2000 Economic Freedom Score	Alesina and Perotti, 1994; Helliwell, 1994; La Porta, Lopez de Silanes, Shleifer, 1999; York, Rosa and Dietz, 2003
Absolute latitude	Acemoglu and Dell, 2010; Acemoglu and Robinson, 2000, 2001, 2006; Acemoglu, 2003, 2005, 2010a, 2010b; Acemoglu, Johnson and Robinson, 2001, 2002, 2005; Easterly, 2000; Poe and Tate, 1994; Ram 1997
Annual population growth rate, 1975-2005 (%)	Acemoglu and Dell, 2010; Acemoglu and Robinson, 2000, 2001, 2006; Acemoglu, 2003, 2005, 2010a, 2010b; Acemoglu, Johnson and Robinson, 2001, 2002, 2005; Crenshaw and Robison, 2010; Ram, 1997
Comparative price levels (US=1.00)	Egert, Drine and Lommatzsch, 2003; Faria and Leon-Ledesma, 2003; Gould, 2002; Kohler and Tausch, 2003; Paya, Venetis and Peel, 2003; Raffer, 1987; Tausch and Ghymers, 2006; Yotopoulos and Sawada, 2005; Yotopoulos, 1996
Foreign savings rate	Bovenberg and van Ewijk, 1997; Cook, 1995; Doucouliagos and Paldam, 2008; Easterly and Schmidthebbel, 1993; Feldstein, 1994; Gine and Townsend, 2004; Singh, 1985; Tausch and Ghymers, 2006; Tausch and Prager, 1993; Taylor, 1992
FPZ (free production zones) employment as % of total population	Chen, 1995; Rondinelli, 1987; Tausch and Ghymers, 2006; Tausch and Prager, 1993
Immigration - Share of population 2005 (%)	Barro and Sala-i-Martin, 2003; Dixon and Moon, 1986, 1989; Dixon, 1987; Durlauf *et al.*, 2008; Fain, 1997; Fosu, 2009, 2010a, 2010b, 2010c; Moon and Dixon, 1992; Shandra et al., 2009; Shandra, 2007a, 2007b; Tausch and Prager, 1993
ln GDP per capita	Afxentiou, 1990a, 1990b; Anand and Ravillion, 1993; Anson, 1988, 1991; Barro, 2000; Cheng, 1989; Dixon and Moon, 1986, 1989; Dixon, 1987; Fosu, 2009, 2010a, 2010b, 2010c; Kakwani, 1993, 1995; Khan, 1991; King, 1998; Knight and Rosa, 2011; Mazumdar, 1996, 2000; Moon and Dixon, 1992; Newman and Thomson, 1989; Rudra, 2009; Selden and Song, 1994; Stern, 2004; Stern, Common and Barboer, 1996; Tausch and Prager, 1993
ln GDP per capita ^2	Afxentiou, 1990a, 1990b; Anand and Ravillion, 1993; Anson, 1988, 1991; Barro, 2000; Cheng, 1989; Dixon and Moon, 1986, 1989; Dixon, 1987; Fosu, 2009, 2010a, 2010b, 2010c; Kakwani, 1993, 1995; Khan, 1991; King, 1998; Knight and Rosa, 2011; Mazumdar, 1996, 2000; Moon and Dixon, 1992; Newman and Thomson, 1989; Rudra, 2009; Selden and Song, 1994; Stern, 2004; Stern, Common and Barboer, 1996; Tausch and Prager, 1993

Table 4. (Continued).

Independent variables, determinants of smart development	Theories or earlier empirical studies, connected with these variables
Membership in the Organization of Islamic Cooperation (OIC)	de Soysa and Ragnhild, 2007; Haynes, 2001
Military expenditures per GDP	Auvinen and Nafziger, 1999; Biswas and Ram, 1986; Brzoska and Lock, 1992; Brzoska and Ohlson, 1986, 1987; Brzoska and Pearson, 1994; Heo, 1998; Mintz and Stevenson, 1995
Military personnel rate ln (MPR+1)	Auvinen and Nafziger, 1999; Heo, 1998; Keller, Poutvaara, and Wagener, 2010; Mintz and Stevenson, 1995; Weede and Jagodzinski, 1980; Weede and Tiefenbach, 1980a, 1980b, 1981; Weede, 1980, 1981a, 1981b, 1983, 1985, 1986, 1993
MNC outward investments (stock) per GDP	Beer, 1999; Bornschier, 1982, 2002; Dick and Jorgenson, 2010; Dutt, 1997; Heshmati, 2006b; Jorgenson and Burns, 2007; Jorgenson, 2003, 2004a, 2004b, 2005, 2006a, 2006b, 2007a, 2007b, 2008, 2009a, 2009b; Jorgenson, and Burns, 2004; Jorgenson, Dick, and Mahutga, 2007; Jorgenson, Kuykendall, and Kennon 2008; Kentor, 1998; Klitgaard and Fedderke, 1995; Lawrence, 2009; Longo and York, 2008; Mostafa and Nataraajan, 2009; Mostafa, 2010a, 2010b; Nugent, and Shandra, 2009; Shandra, 2007a, 2007b; Shandra, and London, 2008; Shandra, Leckband, and London, 2009; Shandra, Leckband, McKinney, and London 2009; Shandra, London, Whooley, and Williamson, 2004; Shandra, Shor, and London, 2008, 2009; Tausch and Prager, 1993; Tausch, 2003; Tsai 1995
MNC PEN - stock of Inward FDI per GDP	Beer, 1999; Bornschier, 1982, 2002; Dick and Jorgenson, 2010; Dutt, 1997; Heshmati, 2006b; Jorgenson and Burns, 2007; Jorgenson, 2003, 2004a, 2004b, 2005, 2006a, 2006b, 2007a, 2007b, 2008, 2009a, 2009b; Jorgenson, and Burns, 2004; Jorgenson, Dick, and Mahutga, 2007; Jorgenson, Kuykendall, and Kennon 2008; Kentor, 1998; Klitgaard and Fedderke, 1995; Lawrence, 2009; Longo and York, 2008; Mostafa and Nataraajan, 2009; Mostafa, 2010a, 2010b; Nugent, and Shandra, 2009; Shandra, 2007a, 2007b; Shandra, and London, 2008; Shandra, Leckband, and London, 2009; Shandra, Leckband, McKinney, and London 2009; Shandra, London, Whooley, and Williamson, 2004; Shandra, Shor, and London, 2008, 2009; Tausch and Prager, 1993; Tausch, 2003; Tsai 1995
MNC PEN: DYN MNC PEN 1995-2005	Beer, 1999; Bornschier, 1982, 2002; Dick and Jorgenson, 2010; Dutt, 1997; Heshmati, 2006b; Jorgenson and Burns, 2007; Jorgenson, 2003, 2004a, 2004b, 2005, 2006a, 2006b, 2007a, 2007b, 2008, 2009a, 2009b; Jorgenson, and Burns, 2004; Jorgenson, Dick, and Mahutga, 2007; Jorgenson, Kuykendall, and

	Kennon 2008; Kentor, 1998; Klitgaard and Fedderke, 1995; Lawrence, 2009; Longo and York, 2008; Mostafa and Nataraajan, 2009; Mostafa, 2010a, 2010b; Nugent, and Shandra, 2009; Shandra, 2007a, 2007b; Shandra, and London, 2008; Shandra, Leckband, and London, 2009; Shandra, Leckband, McKinney, and London 2009; Shandra, London, Whooley, and Williamson, 2004; Shandra, Shor, and London, 2008, 2009; Tausch and Prager, 1993; Tausch, 2003; Tsai 1995
Muslim population share per total population	Acemoglu and Dell, 2010; Acemoglu and Robinson, 2000, 2001, 2006; Acemoglu, 2003, 2005, 2010a, 2010b; Acemoglu, Johnson and Robinson, 2001, 2002, 2005; Ram, 1997
Net international migration rate, 2005-2010	Ehrhardt-Martinez, Crenshaw and Jenkins, 2002
Openness-Index, 1990 (export-share per GDP + import-share per GDP)	Alesina, Spolaore and Wacziarg, 2000; Dollar, 1992a, 1992b; Edwards, 1993; Frankel and Romer, 1999; Rodrik, 2006; Rodrik, Subramanian, and Trebbi, 2004; World Bank, 2005
Population density	Acemoglu and Dell, 2010; Acemoglu and Robinson, 2000, 2001, 2006; Acemoglu, 2003, 2005, 2010a, 2010b; Acemoglu, Johnson and Robinson, 2001, 2002, 2005; Ram, 1997
Public education expenditure per GNP	Blankenau and Simpson, 2004; Glomm and Ravikumar, 1997; Ram, 1986; Scanlan, 2004; Sylwester, 2000; Weede and Kampf, 2002
UNDP education index	Blankenau and Simpson, 2004; Glomm and Ravikumar, 1997; Sylwester, 2000; Weede and Kampf, 2002
Worker remittance inflows as % of GDP	Acosta, Calderon, Fajnzylber, et al., 2008; Amuedo-Dorantes and Pozo, 2004; Martin and Straubhaar, 2002
Years of membership in EMU, 2010	Allsopp and Artis, 2003; Buti, Franco and Ongena, 1998; de la Porte, Pochet and Room, 2001; Egert, Drine and Lommatzsch, 2003; Molle and Boeckhout, 1995
Years of membership in the EU, 2010	Allsopp and Artis, 2003; Buti, Franco and Ongena, 1998; de la Porte, Pochet and Room, 2001; Egert, Drine and Lommatzsch, 2003; Molle and Boeckhout, 1995

The statistical design of our study is thus based on the usual ordinary least square standard regression analysis of the *'kitchen sink type'* (Durlauf *et al.,* 2008; Hertz, Hebert, and Landon, 1994) of economic growth and economic, social and political performance in the research tradition of Barro, 2003.[24] Surveying the vast econometric literature on the subject of the possible drivers and bottlenecks of the EU-2020 process and overall development performance of a given country, one indeed finds support for

[24] To our knowledge, the term 'kitchen sink regression', commonly used in econometrics of economic growth, was re-introduced in more recent standard social science journal vocabulary in Laver and Shepsle, 1999.

the inclusion of geographic and demographic variables in the comparative analysis of development success or failure. Our list is thus corresponding to international research standard praxis in the discipline of general 'development accounting' (Barro and Sala-i-Martin, 2003; Dixon, 1987; Dixon and Moon, 1986, 1989; Durlauf et al., 2008; Fain, 1997; Fosu, 2009, 2010a, 2010b, 2010c; Moon and Dixon, 1992; Shandra, 2007a, 2007b; Shandra et al., 2009; Tausch and Prager, 1993). Compared to a recent approach on the subject (Knight and Rosa, 2011), we do include globalization-oriented variables as well. There is a wide and well-established research tradition in international comparative sociology to include globalization-related drivers of environmental decay (Jorgenson, 2008, 2009a, 2009b, 2009c, 2009d). To exclude such variables and to introduce instead four geographically determined dummy variables (Latin America, former USSR, Africa, and Asia, as was done by Knight and Rosa, 2011) does not necessarily increase the theoretical and predictive power of analysis. Our main independent variables and their theoretical linkages are presented in Table 4.

As to the possible theoretical explanations, we have to state that we regard the openness indicator from a completely different angle as Dollar, 1992 and 1992b: First of all, we show the non-linear trade-off between n-log GDP per capita and economic freedom, showing that almost 45% of economic freedom is being determined by income levels:

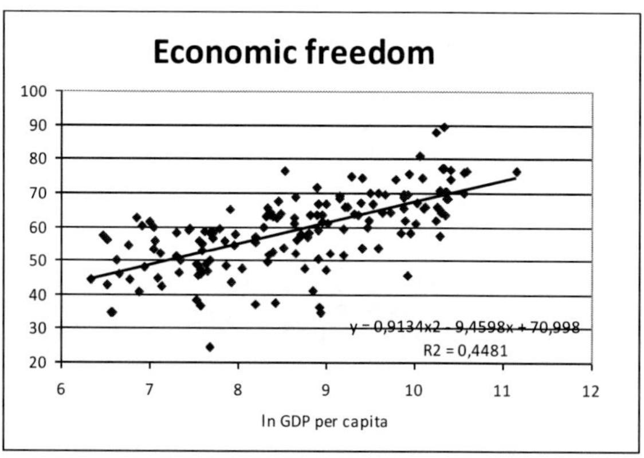

Graph 1. GDP per capita (n-log) and world economic openness.

Table 5. n-log GDP per capita and 'economic freedom'

	ln GDP per capita	2000 Economic Freedom Score	trend value	residual
Hong Kong, China (SAR)	10,34	89,53	69,37	20,16
Singapore	10,24	87,67	68,78	18,88
El Salvador	8,53	76,30	58,00	18,31
Zambia	6,85	62,76	47,47	15,29
New Zealand	10,06	80,89	67,64	13,25
Benin	6,99	61,53	48,39	13,14
Mali	6,91	60,25	47,83	12,42
Malawi	6,47	57,39	45,10	12,29
Chile	9,29	74,68	62,83	11,86
Panama	8,89	71,56	60,31	11,25
Kenya	7,04	59,66	48,67	10,99
Trinidad and Tobago	9,41	74,47	63,54	10,93
Bolivia	7,91	65,03	54,13	10,91
Tanzania	6,51	56,03	45,37	10,67
Jordan	8,45	67,50	57,54	9,96
Peru	8,64	68,67	58,75	9,92
Bahrain	9,94	75,68	66,89	8,79
Jamaica	8,33	65,54	56,80	8,75
Moldova	7,46	59,57	51,28	8,29
Bahamas	9,79	73,86	65,94	7,92
United Kingdom	10,34	77,28	69,37	7,91
Uganda	7,30	58,16	50,30	7,87
Australia	10,32	77,12	69,27	7,85
Senegal	7,45	58,87	51,22	7,65
Madagascar	6,75	54,35	46,87	7,48
Uruguay	9,15	69,33	61,93	7,40
Guatemala	8,37	64,34	57,02	7,32
Switzerland	10,41	76,76	69,80	6,96
Burkina Faso	7,06	55,69	48,82	6,87
United Arab Emirates	10,09	74,23	67,81	6,42
Costa Rica	9,16	68,37	61,97	6,40
Armenia	8,32	63,03	56,70	6,32
Paraguay	8,48	64,01	57,71	6,30
Namibia	8,91	66,73	60,42	6,30
Morocco	8,37	63,25	57,01	6,24
Mongolia	7,63	58,53	52,37	6,16
Sri Lanka	8,39	63,18	57,13	6,04
Argentina	9,50	70,04	64,09	5,95
Cambodia	7,79	59,29	53,40	5,89
Thailand	9,00	66,60	60,97	5,63
United States	10,59	76,42	70,95	5,47
Guinea	7,69	58,18	52,74	5,44

Table 5. (Continued)

	ln GDP per capita	2000 Economic Freedom Score	trend value	residual
Estonia	9,59	69,93	64,66	5,27
Ireland	10,57	76,08	70,82	5,26
Ghana	7,71	58,07	52,91	5,17
Philippines	8,44	62,54	57,44	5,09
Barbados	9,66	69,55	65,14	4,41
Nigeria	7,05	53,13	48,74	4,39
Iceland	10,41	73,97	69,81	4,16
Ethiopia	6,63	50,19	46,09	4,10
Swaziland	8,64	62,58	58,70	3,88
Mauritius	9,39	67,20	63,46	3,74
Kyrgyzstan	7,57	55,70	51,99	3,71
Pakistan	7,71	56,38	52,86	3,52
Malaysia	9,24	65,98	62,47	3,51
Botswana	9,20	65,76	62,27	3,49
Belize	8,82	63,27	59,83	3,44
Ecuador	8,28	59,78	56,49	3,29
Kuwait	9,87	69,71	66,46	3,26
Honduras	7,96	57,62	54,48	3,14
Colombia	8,89	63,33	60,29	3,04
Mozambique	7,12	52,21	49,18	3,03
Korea (Republic of)	9,93	69,70	66,81	2,89
Djibouti	7,60	55,06	52,17	2,88
Turkey	8,96	63,42	60,70	2,72
Saudi Arabia	9,53	66,53	64,33	2,20
Czech Republic	9,87	68,64	66,46	2,17
Samoa	8,63	60,81	58,67	2,14
Papua New Guinea	7,84	55,80	53,70	2,10
Luxembourg	11,16	76,44	74,51	1,92
Japan	10,28	70,71	69,04	1,67
Canada	10,35	70,48	69,46	1,03
Nepal	7,31	51,30	50,35	0,95
Nicaragua	8,20	56,86	55,94	0,91
Netherlands	10,37	70,40	69,56	0,84
South Africa	9,32	63,74	63,01	0,74
Tunisia	8,96	61,35	60,71	0,63
Gambia	7,60	52,71	52,17	0,55
Latvia	9,36	63,38	63,26	0,12
Brazil	9,01	61,10	61,05	0,05
Sierra Leone	6,33	44,24	44,21	0,03
Georgia	7,95	54,34	54,41	-0,07
Myanmar	6,93	47,94	48,01	-0,07
Cyprus	10,03	67,25	67,48	-0,23
Niger	6,66	45,92	46,27	-0,36

	ln GDP per capita	2000 Economic Freedom Score	trend value	residual
Côte d'Ivoire	7,35	50,18	50,60	-0,42
Norway	10,56	70,07	70,76	-0,68
Indonesia	8,19	55,17	55,90	-0,73
Oman	9,63	64,14	64,95	-0,82
Portugal	9,88	65,54	66,53	-0,99
Hungary	9,73	64,38	65,56	-1,18
Austria	10,38	68,40	69,66	-1,26
Denmark	10,37	68,26	69,59	-1,32
Fiji	8,71	57,80	59,16	-1,36
Dominican Republic	8,92	59,03	60,45	-1,42
Gabon	8,80	58,21	59,71	-1,50
Venezuela	8,71	57,43	59,14	-1,71
Lithuania	9,48	61,90	64,00	-2,10
Spain	10,13	65,86	68,06	-2,21
Israel	10,10	65,50	67,90	-2,39
Yemen	6,78	44,50	47,03	-2,54
China	8,68	56,37	58,98	-2,62
Lebanon	8,67	56,13	58,92	-2,79
Burundi	6,52	42,58	45,39	-2,82
Bangladesh	7,53	48,95	51,77	-2,82
Cameroon	7,68	49,89	52,72	-2,83
Mexico	9,19	59,34	62,18	-2,83
Algeria	8,80	56,84	59,69	-2,86
Germany	10,25	65,74	68,83	-3,10
Zimbabwe	7,63	48,67	52,40	-3,73
Sweden	10,29	65,14	69,10	-3,96
Poland	9,47	59,95	63,93	-3,98
Togo	7,34	46,43	50,54	-4,10
Tajikistan	7,09	44,83	49,00	-4,17
Albania	8,51	53,60	57,92	-4,32
Qatar	9,90	62,03	66,60	-4,57
Guyana	8,40	52,42	57,20	-4,78
Finland	10,31	64,34	69,19	-4,85
Sudan	7,58	47,16	52,03	-4,87
Egypt	8,35	51,71	56,87	-5,16
Lesotho	7,87	48,36	53,89	-5,53
Chad	7,64	46,75	52,47	-5,72
Belgium	10,34	63,53	69,42	-5,89
Mauritania	7,57	45,98	52,00	-6,02
Haiti	7,55	45,75	51,85	-6,10
Greece	10,01	60,98	67,31	-6,33
Cape Verde	8,65	51,89	58,80	-6,91
Italy	10,25	61,89	68,80	-6,91
Azerbaijan	8,33	49,83	56,78	-6,95
Rwanda	7,14	42,31	49,31	-7,00

Table 5. (Continued).

	ln GDP per capita	2000 Economic Freedom Score	trend value	residual
Congo	6,89	40,57	47,70	-7,13
India	8,05	47,44	55,03	-7,59
Malta	9,85	58,28	66,29	-8,01
Slovenia	9,95	58,32	66,94	-8,62
Romania	9,05	52,08	61,26	-9,19
Croatia	9,41	53,64	63,54	-9,90
Kazakhstan	8,91	50,35	60,44	-10,09
Russia	9,20	51,84	62,24	-10,40
Vietnam	7,92	43,71	54,18	-10,48
Congo (Democratic Republic of the)	6,56	34,78	45,65	-10,87
Slovakia	9,59	53,77	64,69	-10,92
Guinea-Bissau	6,58	34,73	45,80	-11,07
Ukraine	8,76	47,81	59,49	-11,69
France	10,29	57,36	69,05	-11,69
Bulgaria	9,00	47,34	60,96	-13,62
Uzbekistan	7,53	38,13	51,77	-13,63
Laos	7,58	36,78	52,05	-15,27
Syria	8,19	37,16	55,90	-18,74
Belarus	8,85	41,29	60,03	-18,75
Turkmenistan	8,43	37,60	57,40	-19,80
Equatorial Guinea	9,93	45,62	66,81	-21,19
Iran	8,93	36,11	60,51	-24,40
Libya	8,93	34,65	60,55	-25,90
Angola	7,69	24,27	52,74	-28,47

In Table 5 we show the residuals from a linear trade-off (since, as can be seen by our Graph 3, the curvilinear formulation of the function is not really necessary). Hong Kong, Singapore and El Salvador are – relative to their GDP per capita – the freest economies in the world, while Angola, Libya and Iran are the most unfree economies of the world relative to their GDP per capita.

Table 6. Determinants of economic freedom

Variable	Coefficient	Std Error
% women in government, all levels	0,286**	0,100
Annual population growth rate, 1975-2005 (%)	1,794**	0,634
ln GDP per capita ^2	0,397***	0,041
military personnel rate ln (MPR+1)	-3,21***	1,063

Variable	Coefficient	Std Error
population density	0,008**	0,003
Constant	25,940***	3,639
N =	145	
Adj. R^2 =	52.6%	
F-test =	33.001	
p-value =	0.000	

Significance level: **p* <0.05, ***p* <0.01, ****p* <0.001;

Table 6 now lists the main drivers and bottlenecks of ‘economic freedom’ on the basis of our independent variables. Our results were achieved with 145 countries of the world with complete data. Our regression explains 52.6% of the variance of ‘economic freedom’. Independent of the income effect on ‘economic freedom’, which, in numerical terms is quite strong and which is statistically highly significant, we find rather surprisingly no significant relationship with ‘world economic openness’ (as would have been to have to be expected by Dollar, 1992a, and 1992b, and all subsequent investigations of the ‘world economically open growth is good for the poor’ paradigm. By contrast, we have to propose a peace research paradigm of world economic openness because we find that military personnel ratios are the biggest bottleneck for economic freedom; and that institutional feminism is not an adversary, but an ally of economic freedom! In addition, we also find that the demographic challenges, posed by population growth and population density are the healthiest impulses for a society to embrace economic freedom, independent of the level of incomes achieved, independent of the level of feminism in power, and independent of the military personnel ratio. All the ‘world economic variables’ and other possible drivers and bottlenecks of economic freedom wield only insignificant results. Among them are the following variables:

- % world population
- Absolute latitude
- comparative price levels (US=1.00)
- foreign savings rate
- FPZ (free production zones) employment as % of total population
- ln GDP per capita

- Membership in the Islamic Conference
- military personnel rate ln (MPR+1)
- MNC outward investments (stock) per GDP
- MNC PEN - stock of Inward FDI per GDP
- MNC PEN: DYN MNC PEN 1995-2005
- Openness-Index, 1990 (export-share per GDP + import-share per GDP)
- public education expenditure per GNP
- UNDP education index

The choice of a country to be included in the final analysis (175 countries) was determined by the availability of fairly good data series for these independent variables (if not mentioned otherwise, UNDP data for the middle of the first decade of the new millenium).

The statistical design of our study is based on the usual, IBM SPSS XXIV[25] ordinary least square standard regression of the 'kitchen sink type' (Durlauf *et al.,* 2008; Hertz, Hebert, and Landon, 1994) of economic growth and economic, social and political performance in the research tradition of Barro, 2003. To our knowledge, the term *'kitchen sink regression',* commonly used in econometrics of economic growth, was re-introduced in more recent standard social science journal vocabulary in Laver and Shepsle, 1999. Prior stepwise regression procedures selected the significant among the total list of 26 available predictors. Among the many international studies, applying such a research design, we find Hertz, Hebert, and Landon, 1994. This study analysed the effects of independent variables including dietary factors, medical resource availability, gross national product (GNP/capita), literacy rates, growth in the labour force, and provision of sanitation facilities and safe water on infant and maternal mortality rates and life expectancy at birth. The study fitted a series of general linear models for each of the three dependent variables[26].

---

[25] http://www-01.ibm.com/software/analytics/spss/products/statistics/

[26] It emerged that the percent of households without sanitation facilities showed the strongest association with all three dependent variables: life expectancy at birth, infant mortality rate, and maternal mortality rate.

Since our book does not feature primarily on ecological footprint, but on a variety of measures of 'smart development', which are mathematically derived from the logic of the Happy Planet Index (see also Ng, 2008a and 2008b; Veenhoven, 1996), it suffices to say here that ecological footprint (g ha/cap)[27], as it is universally well-known by now, is indeed a one-catch all-indicator of ecological strain, caused by human activity. Ecological footprint and its measurement cannot be further debated in the framework of our book and at this stage must be regarded as a 'given' (for studies about the logic and determinants of footprint per capita see also Dietz *et al.*, 2007 and 2009). It should be enough to state here that it is measure of the amount of land required to provide for all their resource requirements plus the amount of vegetated land required to sequester (absorb) all their CO2 emissions and the CO2 emissions embodied in the products individuals consume. This figure is expressed in units of 'global hectares'. In 2005, the per capita footprint for the rich OECD nations was 6.0 global hectares[28]. The other variables are then compared to the footprint, which was used by a society to achieve a given standard of democracy, economic growth, gender equality, human development, research and development, and social cohesion. We should also remind our readers here of the fact that the Happy Planet Index Organization measures the Happy Planet Index on the basis of the global life satisfaction (Happy Life Years), which have to be maximized in relationship to the 'ecological price' of happiness, ecological footprint.

It is then of course very tempting to calculate – in a Schumacherian tradition – the 'environmental price' of different development processes, like democracy, economic growth, gender equality, human development, research and development, and social cohesion. The Happy Planet Organisation calculates the HPI in the following way:

$$HPI_i = \left((HLYE_i)/(EFPC_i + \alpha)\right) \times \beta \tag{1}$$

[27] http://www.footprintnetwork.org/en/index.php/GFN/
[28] http://www.happyplanetindex.org/

where Happy Life Years (HLYE) is obtained as the product of life expectancy (LE) and average life satisfaction (LS) index. In its currently used formula, the Happy Planet Organization adds a constant (α) to ecological footprint. The result of the division: [Happy Life Years divided by Ecological Footprint plus the constant (α)] is then multiplied by another, equally arbitrarily chosen constant (β) to normalize the efficiency index. In the Happy Planet Organization formula, the constants have the following numerical values: (α) = 3.35 and (β) = 6.42.

The highest global HPI score is that of Costa Rica (76.1 out of 100). Of the 10 best performing countries of the world, nine are in Latin America.[29] But unfortunately, the Happy Planet Organization's straightforward and simple methodology overlooks advances in the social sciences, which long ago already developed appropriate methodologies to relate life quality variables – like life expectancy – to GDP per capita or energy consumption levels in empirical, and non-linear mathematical formulations, which capture much better than the above simple equation the underlying non-linear tradeoffs between *'energy consumption and/or environmental strain'* and *'life quality'* (Goldstein, 1985). Goldstein's empirically developed idea that basic human needs indicators – like life expectancy – are a non-linear function of development levels has been so widely received in the social science literature that is has become a real international standard nowadays (see Afxentiou, 1990a, 1990b; Anand and Ravillion, 1993; Anson, 1988, 1991; Cheng, 1989; Dixon, 1987; Dixon and Moon, 1986, 1989; Fosu, 2009, 2010a, 2010b, 2010c; Kakwani, 1993, 1995; Khan, 1991; King, 1998; Knight and Rosa, 2011; Mazumdar, 1996, 2000; Moon and Dixon, 1992; Newman and Thomson, 1989; Rudra, 2009; Tausch and Prager, 1993). The neglect of such a basic non-linear function (whatever its concrete mathematical formulation[30]) is a major shortcoming of the currently used Happy Planet Index calculation. The global public health research tradition, too, produced massive evidence on the cross-national determinants of life expectancy and other life quality variables (to quote but a few studies:

[29] http://www.happyplanetindex.org/

[30] The most often encountered formulation in the literature is a double logarithmic expression, based on the natural logarithm of development level/energy consumption and its square.

Wilkinson, 1992; Wilkinson and Picket, 2006; Tausch, 2010). This growing methodological convergence of the social sciences, geography and earth sciences, and public health research on predictors of life quality at different stages of development should be taken into account in this book (Fain, et al. 1997; Mostafa, 2010a and 2010b; Mostafa and Nataraajan, 2009; Shandra, 2007a, 2007b, Shandra, Leckband, McKinney and London, 2009). Graph 2 depicts the trade-off between ecological footprint and happy life years; the (standardized) residuals in our graph are a reformulated Happy Planet Index (see Graph 2).

In a similar vein, we investigated the non-linear trade-offs between ecological footprint and the combined UNDP type indices for six dimensions of development, derived from freely available current cross-national, comparative data (see Table 7).

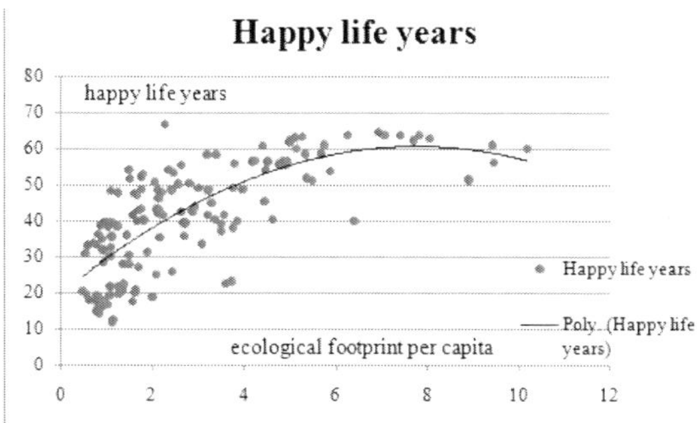

Variable	Coefficient	Std Error
Ecological Footprint per capita	10.541***	1.313
Ecological Footprint per capita^2	–0.677***	0.147
Constant	19.631***	2.246
N =	140	
Adj. R^2 =	54.1%	
F-test =	83.081	
p-value =	0.000	

Significance level: *p <0.05, **p <0.01, ***p <0.001;

Graph 2. The non-linear relationship between Happy Life Years (HLYE, vertical Y) and ecological footprint (horizontal X), n = 140 countries in 2005

Graphs 3a – 3g show the trade-off between ecological footprint and ‘smart development’, measured for the various dimensions (democracy, economic growth, gender equality, human development, research and development, social cohesion, and the two differently combined overall measurement scales). Only the scatterplot for ecological footprint and 'social cohesion' suggests a weaker relationship, all the other relationships are considerable. The overall development performance, democracy, gender equality, human development, research and development are a clear non-linear, inverted U-shaped function of ecological footprint per capita, while economic growth and also social cohesion first decrease and then increase with rising levels of ecological footprint per capita.

Table 7. The combined six components, measuring development, and the overall indicators, combining 26 variables

democracy	Combined Failed States Index
democracy	Civil and Political Liberties violations
democracy	Corruption avoidance measure
democracy	Democracy measure
democracy	Global tolerance index
democracy	Rule of law
economic growth	Crisis Performance Factor
economic growth	Economic growth IMF prediction growth rate in 2009
economic growth	Economic growth IMF prediction growth rate in 2010
economic growth	Economic growth in real terms pc. per annum, 1990-2005
Gender equality	Closing economic gender gap
Gender equality	Closing educational gender gap
Gender equality	Closing health and survivial gender gap
Gender equality	Closing of global gender gap overall score 2009
Gender equality	Closing political gender gap
Gender equality	Gender empowerment index value
human development	Infant mortality 2005
human development	Female survival probability of surviving to age 65 female
human development	Human development index (HDI) value 2004
human development	Life Expectancy (years)
human development	Life Satisfaction (0-10)
R&D	Country share in top world 500 Universities
R&D	Per capita world class universities

R&D	Tertiary enrollment
social cohesion	Quintile share income difference between richest and poorest 20%
social cohesion	Unemployment rate
nonparametric_26 equal weights	Overall 26 development index
nonparametric, weighting each dimension equally	Overall 26 development index, based on six dimensions

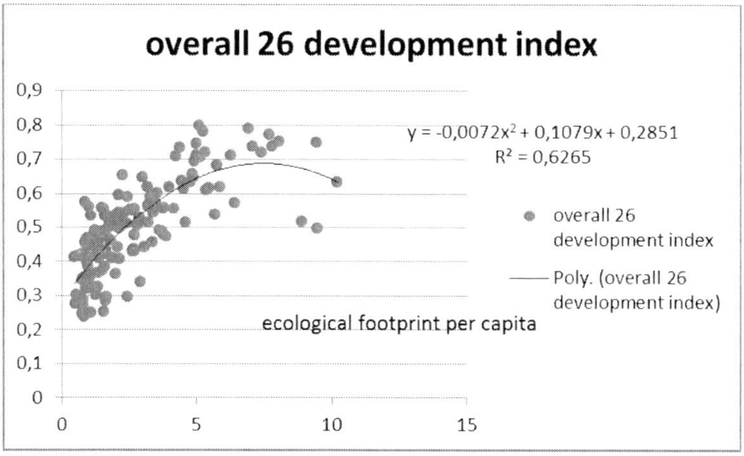

Graph 3a. Ecological footprint and the general development performance index, based on an equal weighting of its 26 components.

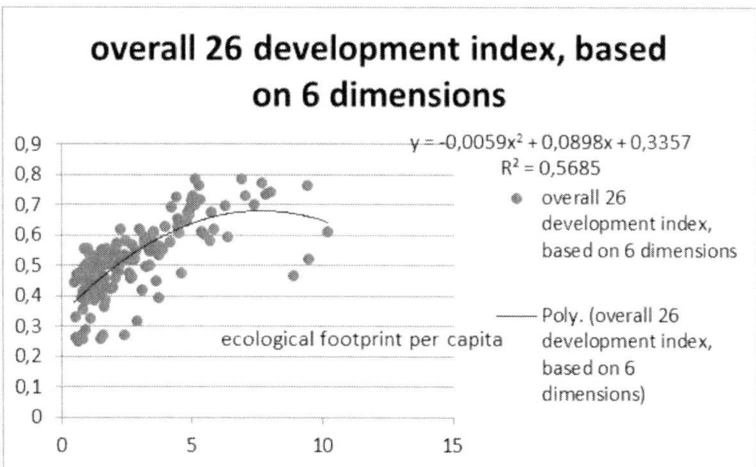

Graph 3b. Ecological footprint and the general development performance index, based on an equal weighting of the six dimensions, underlying the 26 components.

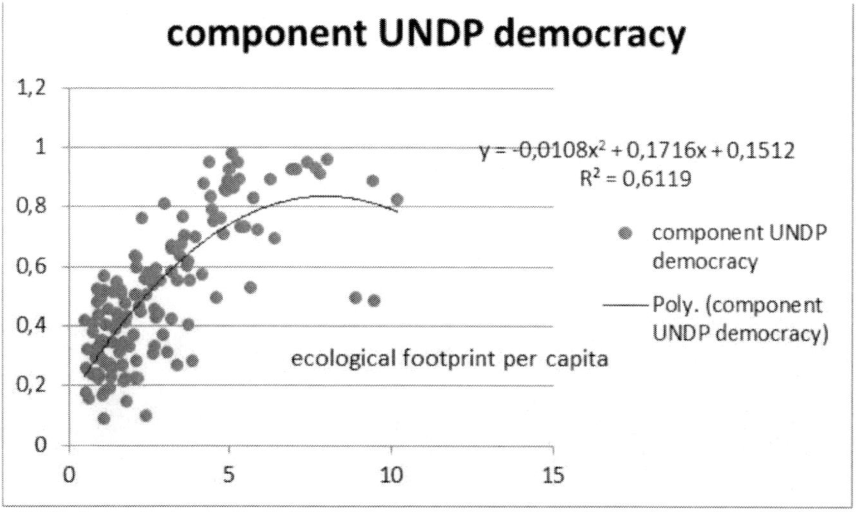

Graph 3c. Ecological footprint and democratic performance (6 components combined).

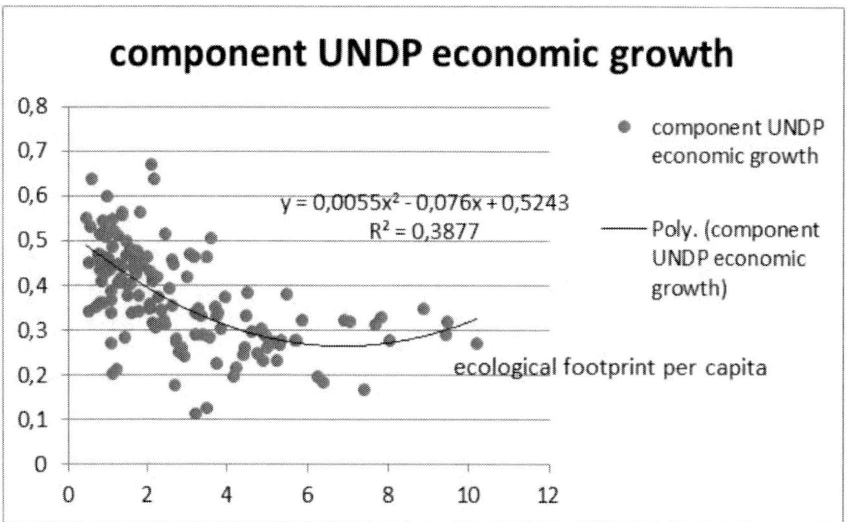

Graph 3d. Ecological footprint and economic growth performance (4 components combined).

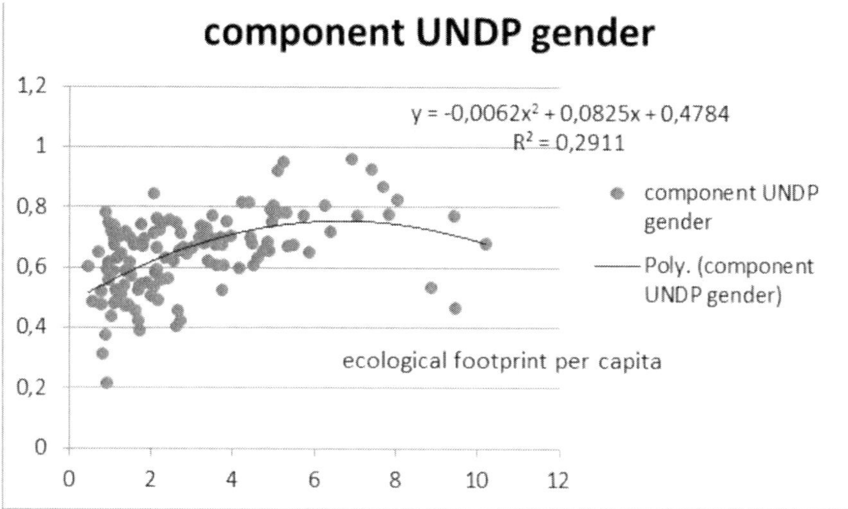

Graph 3e. Ecological footprint and gender equality performance (6 components combined).

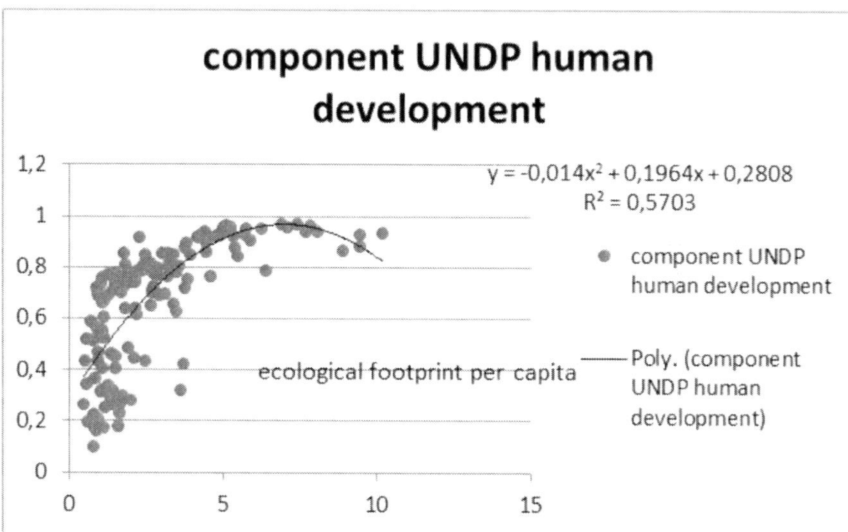

Graph 3f. Ecological footprint and human development performance (5 components combined).

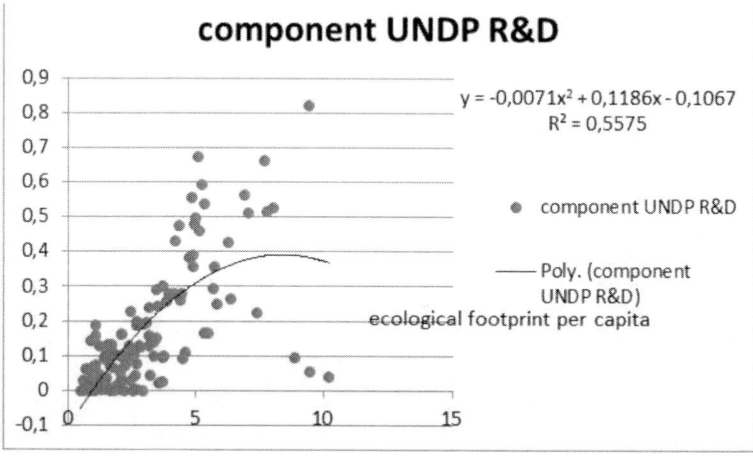

Graph 3g. Ecological footprint and research and development performance (3 components combined).

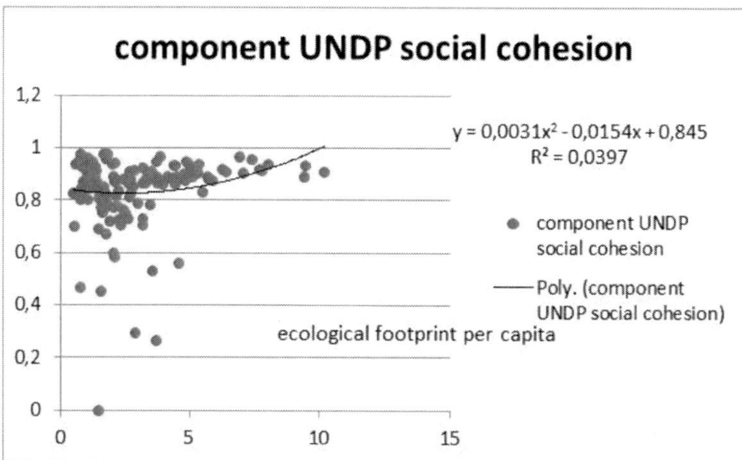

Graph 3h. Ecological footprint and social cohesion performance (2 components combined).

As we already explained, the hitherto existing calculations of the HPI[31], provided by the Happy Planet Organization, are merely based on simple arithmetical principles.

[31] Although we presume the main contemporary global environment indicators to be known, we refer our readers especially to the very comprehensive Yale/Columbia environmental data

Following Heintz, 1972 we propose as an alternative method a residual method, and calculate our smart development indicators as the standardized residuals from Graph 3. The standardized residual values are computed as observed minus predicted development outcomes divided by the square root of the residual mean square (see Appendix, Table 1 and 2):

$$SDP_i = (HLYE_i - H\hat{LYE}_i) / \hat{\sigma} \tag{2}$$

High positive outlayers imply a very high smart development performance, while countries below the trend line are the countries with a low smart development performance. Having established a residual-based smart Development Indicator family, we now can look more realistically at the cross-national determinants of smart development performance.

series, available at http://sedac.ciesin.columbia.edu/es/esi/ and http://epi.yale.edu/Home . The important new 'grammar' of the global footprint discourse can be found at http://www.footprintnetwork.org/en/index.php/GFN/page/glossary/.

Chapter 3

RESULTS ON THE DRIVERS AND BOTTLENECKS OF 'SMART DEVELOPMENT'

The image of social realities suggested upon a very first inspection of smart development performance values around the globe would suggest a Friedrich August Hayek vision (Hayek, 1945, 1989) of markets, inequality and a free society interacting with one another. There should be no blocks against inequalities in the name of whatever 'social justice', explaining then the phenomenal success of the unequal Latin American societies on the parameters of smart development (see especially, the global rankings of smart development in Table 3 of the Appendix). A the same time, the high-equality performers in global society (quintile share of less than 5.0) with a relatively high per-capita income are at the same time bad performers on the new smart development scales. Notably enough, several of these countries are members of the European Union and traditional developed western welfare states. This very first glance at the data would suggest a complete turn-around from the 'European social model' (Tausch and Ghymers, 2006) in favour of a high-inequality, open to globalization 'Latin American model' or Philippine model as the best way to achieve a good 'smart development' performance. However, such a first glance completely overlooks the massive available evidence about world economic openness and the failure of 'smart development'.

As to multivariate analysis, first preliminary stepwise regression procedures with mean substitution of missing variables revealed a re-current pattern of the importance and predictive capability robustness of the chosen variables among the 26 independent variables with a theoretically well-plausible greater and significant effect on the dependent variables (the six component indicators of development and the overall development performance indicators. The final results were achieved by forward multiple regression based on list wise deletion of missing values, and based exclusively on the significant predictors from the prior preliminary stepwise regressions. We first present, variable by variable, and driver by driver, and bottleneck by bottleneck, the significant results of our multiple regression analyses (standardized regression coefficients and their significance):

The following independent variables *wield only 'good' and positive effects on smart development:*

- % women in government, all levels (feminist theory; three effects positive; zero effects negative)
- % world population (Amin's five monopolies of power; three effects positive; zero effects negative)
- Economic Freedom Score (Amin's critique of rent-seeking; three effects positive; zero effects negative)
- MNC outward investments (stock) per GDP (Bornschier's dependency theory; one effect positive; zero effects negative)
- population density (José Carlos Mariategui's dependency theory; one effect positive; zero effects negative)
- UNDP education index (Steindl/Kalecki-paradigm; two effects positive; zero effects negative)
- Years of membership in the EU (Amin's theory about the role of integration; one effect positive; zero effects negative)

Table 8. The significant drivers and bottlenecks of smart development

Independent Variable	Dependent variable	Beta	Error probability
% women in government, all levels (feminist theory, stressing the need to feminize structures of government)	overall smart development index, based on 26 variables, weighted equally	0,185	0,045
% women in government, all levels (feminist theory, stressing the need to feminize structures of government)	Smart democracy	0,196	0,007
% women in government, all levels (feminist theory, stressing the need to feminize structures of government)	Smart gender justice	0,300	0,001
% world population (Amin's five monopolies of power)	Smart human development	0,152	0,061
% world population (Amin's five monopolies of power)	Happy Life Years	0,161	0,060
% world population (Amin's five monopolies of power)	Smart economic growth	0,261	0,002
2000 Economic Freedom Score (its absence is explained either by Amin's critique of rent-seeking seeking in the periphery versus conventional neo-liberal theories of economic growth)	overall smart development index, based on 26 variables, weighted equally	0,336	0,002
2000 Economic Freedom Score (its absence is explained either by Amin's critique of rent-seeking seeking in the periphery versus conventional neo-liberal theories of economic growth)	overall smart development index, based on 26 variables, weighting equally the six component dimensions	0,402	0,000
2000 Economic Freedom Score (its absence is explained either by Amin's critique of rent-seeking seeking in the periphery versus conventional neo-liberal theories of economic growth)	Smart democracy	0,457	0,000
Absolute latitude (Andre Gunder Frank's 'Re-Orient' model)	Smart economic growth	-0,234	0,006
Annual population growth rate, 1975-2005 (%) (Paul Israel Singer's dependency theory)	Smart R&D	-0,253	0,007
Annual population growth rate, 1975-2005 (%) (Paul Israel Singer's dependency theory)	Smart social cohesion	-0,248	0,006
Immigration - Share of population 2005 (%) (Amin's theory about the role of migration)	Smart democracy	-0,348	0,000

Table 8. (Continued).

Independent Variable	Dependent variable	Beta	Error probability
military expenditures per GDP (quantitative dependency and peace research approaches)	Happy Life Years	-0,245	0,004
military expenditures per GDP (quantitative dependency and peace research approaches)	Smart gender justice	-0,204	0,018
military expenditures per GDP (quantitative dependency and peace research approaches)	overall smart development index, based on 26 variables, weighted equally	-0,191	0,021
military expenditures per GDP (quantitative dependency and peace research approaches)	overall smart development index, based on 26 variables, weighting equally the six component dimensions	-0,166	0,074
military personnel rate ln (quantitative dependency and peace research approaches)	Smart democracy	-0,221	0,002
MNC outward investments (stock) per GDP (Bornschier's dependency theory, stressing the importance of MNC headquarter status in international society)	Smart R&D	0,479	0,000
Muslim population share per total population (Amin's critique of Islamism, implicitly expecting a negative trade-off with development performance versus Andre Gunder Frank's 'Re-Orient' model, expecting a transfer of growth and productive activities to the global East and South)	Smart gender justice	-0,396	0,000
Muslim population share per total population (Amin's critique of Islamism, implicitly expecting a negative trade-off with development performance versus Andre Gunder Frank's 'Re-Orient' model, expecting a transfer of growth and productive activities to the global East and South)	Smart economic growth	0,313	0,000
Openness-Index, 1990 (export-share per GDP + import-share per GDP) (Amin's conception of the role of the peripheries)	Smart R&D	-0,552	0,000

Independent Variable	Dependent variable	Beta	Error probability
Openness-Index, 1990 (export-share per GDP + import-share per GDP) (Amin's conception of the role of the peripheries)	overall smart development index, based on 26 variables, weighting equally the six component dimensions	-0,222	0,019
Openness-Index, 1990 (export-share per GDP + import-share per GDP) (Amin's conception of the role of the peripheries)	overall smart development index, based on 26 variables, weighted equally	-0,170	0,048
population density (José Carlos Mariategui's dependency theory)	overall smart development index, based on 26 variables, weighted equally	0,214	0,010
public education expenditure per GNP (human capital approaches in the tradition of the UNDP versus Kalecki/Steindl paradigm versus neo-liberal approaches, featuring a 'crowding out' phenomenon)	Smart social cohesion	-0,270	0,003
public education expenditure per GNP (human capital approaches in the tradition of the UNDP versus Kalecki/Steindl paradigm versus neo-liberal approaches, featuring a 'crowding out' phenomenon)	Smart human development	-0,196	0,024
public education expenditure per GNP (human capital approaches in the tradition of the UNDP versus Kalecki/Steindl paradigm versus neo-liberal approaches, featuring a 'crowding out' phenomenon)	Smart R&D	0,235	0,010
UNDP education index (human capital approaches in the tradition of the UNDP versus Kalecki/Steindl paradigm)	overall smart development index, based on 26 variables, weighted equally	0,198	0,036
UNDP education index (human capital approaches in the tradition of the UNDP versus Kalecki/Steindl paradigm)	Smart human development	0,478	0,000
worker remittance inflows as % of GDP (conventional centre-periphery models about the negative consequences of the brain drain versus 'new migration theories', underlining the positive effects of worker remittances on migration sending countries)	Smart economic growth	-0,262	0,002
worker remittance inflows as % of GDP (conventional centre-periphery models about the negative consequences of the brain drain versus 'new migration theories', underlining the positive effects of worker remittances on migration sending countries)	overall smart development index, based on 26 variables, weighting equally the six component dimensions	0,177	0,064

Table 8. (Continued).

Independent Variable	Dependent variable	Beta	Error probability
worker remittance inflows as % of GDP (conventional centre-periphery models about the negative consequences of the brain drain versus 'new migration theories', underlining the positive effects of worker remittances on migration sending countries)	overall smart development index, based on 26 variables, weighted equally	0,208	0,016
worker remittance inflows as % of GDP (conventional centre-periphery models about the negative consequences of the brain drain versus 'new migration theories', underlining the positive effects of worker remittances on migration sending countries)	Smart R&D	0,229	0,017
worker remittance inflows as % of GDP (conventional centre-periphery models about the negative consequences of the brain drain versus 'new migration theories', underlining the positive effects of worker remittances on migration sending countries)	Smart gender justice	0,241	0,007
worker remittance inflows as % of GDP (conventional centre-periphery models about the negative consequences of the brain drain versus 'new migration theories', underlining the positive effects of worker remittances on migration sending countries)	Happy Life Years	0,288	0,002
worker remittance inflows as % of GDP (conventional centre-periphery models about the negative consequences of the brain drain versus 'new migration theories', underlining the positive effects of worker remittances on migration sending countries)	Smart human development	0,352	0,000
Years of membership in the EU, 2010 (Amin's theory about the importance of European integration as a counterweight to US dominance in the world system)	Smart democracy	0,183	0,006

Table 9. Results well compatible with a re-formulated globalization critical paradigm

Theory	Independent Variable	Dependent variable	Beta	Error probability
Andre Gunder Frank	Absolute latitude (Andre Gunder Frank's 'Re-Orient' model)	Smart economic growth	-0,234	0,006
Andre Gunder Frank	Muslim population share per total population (Andre Gunder Frank's 'Re-Orient' model)	Smart economic growth	0,313	0,000
Samir Amin	% world population (Amin's five monopolies of power)	Smart human development	0,152	0,061
Samir Amin	% world population (Amin's five monopolies of power)	Happy Life Years	0,161	0,060
Samir Amin	% world population (Amin's five monopolies of power)	Smart economic growth	0,261	0,002
Samir Amin	2000 Economic Freedom Score (Amin's critique of rent-seeking)	overall smart development index, based on 26 variables, weighted equally	0,336	0,002
Samir Amin	2000 Economic Freedom Score (Amin's critique of rent-seeking)	overall smart development index, based on 26 variables, weighting equally the six component dimensions	0,402	0,000
Samir Amin	2000 Economic Freedom Score (Amin's critique of rent-seeking)	Smart democracy	0,457	0,000
Samir Amin	Immigration - Share of population 2005 (%) (Amin's theory about the role of migration)	Smart democracy	-0,348	0,000
Samir Amin	Muslim population share per total population (Amin's critique of Islamism)	Smart gender justice	-0,396	0,000
Samir Amin	Openness-Index, 1990 (export-share per GDP + import-share per GDP) (Amin's conception of the role of the peripheries)	Smart R&D	-0,552	0,000

Table 9. (Continued).

Theory	Independent Variable	Dependent variable	Beta	Error probability
Samir Amin	Openness-Index, 1990 (export-share per GDP + import-share per GDP) (Amin's conception of the role of the peripheries)	overall smart development index, based on 26 variables, weighting equally the six component dimensions	-0,222	0,019
Samir Amin	Openness-Index, 1990 (export-share per GDP + import-share per GDP) (Amin's conception of the role of the peripheries)	overall smart development index, based on 26 variables, weighted equally	-0,170	0,048
Samir Amin	worker remittance inflows as % of GDP (Amin's theory about the role of migration)	overall smart development index, based on 26 variables, weighting equally the six component dimensions	0,177	0,064
Samir Amin	worker remittance inflows as % of GDP (Amin's theory about the role of migration)	overall smart development index, based on 26 variables, weighted equally	0,208	0,016
Samir Amin	worker remittance inflows as % of GDP (Amin's theory about the role of migration)	Smart R&D	0,229	0,017
Samir Amin	worker remittance inflows as % of GDP (Amin's theory about the role of migration)	Smart gender justice	0,241	0,007
Samir Amin	worker remittance inflows as % of GDP (Amin's theory about the role of migration)	Happy Life Years	0,288	0,002
Samir Amin	worker remittance inflows as % of GDP (Amin's theory about the role of migration)	Smart human development	0,352	0,000
Samir Amin	Years of membership in the EU, 2010 (Amin's theory about the role of integration)	Smart democracy	0,183	0,006
Volker Bornschier	MNC outward investments (stock) per GDP (Bornschier's dependency theory)	Smart R&D	0,479	0,000
brain drain theories	worker remittance inflows as % of GDP (conventional centre-periphery models about the negative consequences of the brain drain)	Smart economic growth	-0,262	0,002

Theory	Independent Variable	Dependent variable	Beta	Error probability
feminism	% women in government, all levels (feminist theory)	overall smart development index, based on 26 variables, weighted equally	0,185	0,045
feminism	% women in government, all levels (feminist theory)	Smart democracy	0,196	0,007
feminism	% women in government, all levels (feminist theory)	Smart gender justice	0,300	0,001
José Carlos Mariategui	population density (José Carlos Mariategui's dependency theory)	overall smart development index, based on 26 variables, weighted equally	0,214	0,010
peace research	military expenditures per GDP (dependency and peace research approaches)	Happy Life Years	-0,245	0,004
peace research	military expenditures per GDP (dependency and peace research approaches)	Smart gender justice	-0,204	0,018
peace research	military expenditures per GDP (dependency and peace research approaches)	overall smart development index, based on 26 variables, weighted equally	-0,191	0,021
peace research	military expenditures per GDP (dependency and peace research approaches)	overall smart development index, based on 26 variables, weighting equally the six component dimensions	-0,166	0,074
peace research	military personnel rate ln (dependency and peace research approaches)	Smart democracy	-0,221	0,002
Paul Israel Singer	Annual population growth rate, 1975-2005 (%) (Paul Israel Singer's dependency theory)	Smart R&D	-0,253	0,007
Paul Israel Singer	Annual population growth rate, 1975-2005 (%) (Paul Israel Singer's dependency theory)	Smart social cohesion	-0,248	0,006
Joseph Steindl	public education expenditure per GNP (Steindl/Kalecki-paradigm)	Smart R&D	0,235	0,010
Joseph Steindl	UNDP education index (Steindl/Kalecki-paradigm)	overall smart development index, based on 26 variables, weighted equally	0,198	0,036
Joseph Steindl	UNDP education index (Steindl/Kalecki-paradigm)	Smart human development	0,478	0,000

The *following predictors wielded only negative consequences on smart development:*

- Absolute latitude (Andre Gunder Frank's *'Re-Orient'* model; zero effects positive; one effect negative)
- Annual population growth rate (%) (Paul Israel Singer's dependency theory; zero effects positive; two effects negative)
- Immigration share of total population (%) (Amin's theory about the role of migration; zero effects positive; one effect negative)
- military expenditures per GDP (dependency and peace research approaches; zero effects positive; four effects negative)
- military personnel rate (dependency and peace research approaches; zero effects positive; one effect negative)
- Openness-Index (export-share per GDP minus import-share per GDP) (Amin's conception of the role of the peripheries; zero effects positive, three effects negative)

The following variables wielded mixed results:

- worker remittance inflows as % of GDP (six effects positive; one effect negative)
- Muslim population shares (one effect positive; one effect negative)
- public education expenditure per GNP (one effect positive; two effects negative)

The power, wielded by the predictors

- workers remittances (six positive effects);
- feminization of power structure (three positive effects)
- share of world population (three positive effects)
- economic freedom (three positive effects)
- world economic openness index (three negative effects),
- military expenditures (four negative effects);

seems to be overwhelming.

Table 9 now summarizes our results from the viewpoint of the theories presented in Chapter 2. Only the negative effects, wielded by public education expenditure per GNP on smart social cohesion and on smart human development cannot be properly explained as yet by globalization critical theories, presented above, suggesting rather the existence of strong crowding-out effects of public education expenditures on smart redistribution and smart human development.

Table 10. The drivers and bottlenecks of Happy Planet performance

Independent Variable	B	Standard error	Beta	t-value	Error probability
Constant	-124.628	42.647		-2.922	0.004
% world population	0.596	0.313	0.161	1.904	0.060
ln GDP per capita	26.062	10.069	3.136	2.588	0.011
ln GDP per capita ^2	-1.309	0.584	-2.731	-2.241	0.027
military expenditures per GDP	-1.098	0.376	-0.245	-2.922	0.004
worker remittance inflows as % of GDP	0.420	0.133	0.288	3.153	0.002
memorandum item: statistical properties of the equation	adj R^2	df	F	error probability of the entire equation	
	29.000	102	9.339	.000	

In the following, we will present, equation by equation, the results of our research. Table 10 shows the significant drivers and bottlenecks of Happy Planet performance, i.e. happy life years in relationship to the ecological footprint of a society used. The z-standardized residuals from Graph 3 are well-explained; our equation is based on 103 countries with complete data. Our equation explains 29% of total variance, the F-value for the entire equation is 9.339, and the error probability is .000. The constant is -124.628 and is significant. There is a clear 'Kuznets' curve at work (see also Stern, 2004). But the shape of the curve contradicts much of the earlier debate on the subject: with rising per capita incomes, problem solving capacities first increase and then decrease. The larger states in the world system, having a larger share of global population, are much better able to achieve a good happy life years performance at relatively low ecological costs, measured in ecological footprints than smaller nations. This clearly contradicts the 'small is beautiful' philosophy in the tradition of Kohr and Schumacher. Military expenditures are a clear additional burden on an ecologically viable happy planet performance, while societies, depending on worker remittances, clearly manage to perform better on this scale than other societies around the globe.

Table 11. Drivers and bottlenecks of smart overall development

Independent Variable	B	Standard error	Beta	t-value	Error probability
Constant	-2.486	0.533		-4.666	0.000
% women in government. all levels	0.025	0.012	0.185	2.027	0.045
2000 Economic Freedom Score	0.031	0.010	0.336	3.239	0.002
military expenditures per GDP	-0.076	0.032	-0.191	-2.345	0.021
Openness-Index. 1990 (export-share per GDP + import-share per GDP)	-0.004	0.002	-0.170	-2.007	0.048
population density	0.002	0.001	0.214	2.612	0.010
UNDP education index	0.945	0.445	0.198	2.123	0.036
worker remittance inflows as % of GDP	0.027	0.011	0.208	2.459	0.016
memorandum item: statistical properties of the equation	adj R^2	df	F	error probability of the entire equation	
	37.000	100	9.392	.000	

In a similar fashion, we can establish in Table 11 that in the 101 countries with complete data, smart overall development, as defined in Graph 3a of this work, is explained to 37% by our model. The F-test for the entire equation is 9.392, the error probability is .000. The constant is -2.486 and is significant. The ten countries of the world system, best combining the performance on our 26 development indicators and avoiding ecological footprint at the same time are the Philippines; Sri Lanka; Costa Rica; Sweden; Jamaica; Dominican Republic; Finland; Peru; Netherlands; and Trinidad and Tobago. The ten worst performers on this scale are Sudan; Bosnia and Herzegovina; Central African Republic; United Arab Emirates; Niger; Kuwait; Chad; Zimbabwe; Burundi; and Hong Kong, China (SAR). Feminism in power, economic freedom, population density, the UNDP education index as well as the receipt of worker remittances all significantly contribute towards a smart overall development, while high military expenditures and a high world economic openness are a bottleneck for 'smart overall development'.

Table 12. Drivers and bottlenecks of smart overall development, based on an index, which weights the six dimensions equally

Independent Variable	B	standard error	Beta	t-value	error probability
Constant	-1.469	0.536		-2.741	0.007
2000 Economic Freedom Score	0.035	0.008	0.402	4.158	0.000
military expenditures per GDP	-0.061	0.034	-0.166	-1.808	0.074
Openness-Index. 1990 (export-share per GDP + import-share per GDP)	-0.005	0.002	-0.222	-2.376	0.019
worker remittance inflows as % of GDP	0.021	0.011	0.177	1.871	0.064
memorandum item: statistical properties of the equation	adj R^2	df	F	error probability of the entire equation	
	19.000	101	6.908	.000	

Also, it emerges that the results about the drivers of overall *smart development performance* are similar to the ones, reported in Table 11, if we calculate the overall development performance by *weighting equally its six component indices* and only then calculating the overall final country performance score, and not, unlike in Table 11, being the sum of the equally weighted 26 original component indices (as to the trade-off with ecological footprint, see Graph 3b of this work). Economic freedom, and received worker remittances per GDP again emerge as the 'drivers' of smart development (Table 12), while the bottlenecks of smart overall development performance are again military expenditures per GDP and world economic openness. This time, the adjusted R^2 is 19%, and the equation is based on 102 countries with complete data. The F-test for the entire equation is 6.908, and the equation is significant at the .000-level. The constant is -1.469 and is significant.

Table 13. Drivers and bottlenecks of smart democracy

Independent Variable	B	Standard error	Beta	t-value	Error probability
Constant	-2.037	0.409		-4.978	0.000
% women in government. all levels	0.029	0.011	0.196	2.753	0.007
2000 Economic Freedom Score	0.041	0.007	0.457	5.826	0.000
military personnel rate ln (MPR+1)	-0.334	0.105	-0.221	-3.162	0.002
Immigration - Share of population 2005 (%)	-0.031	0.007	-0.348	-4.549	0.000
Years of membership in the EU. 2010	0.014	0.005	0.183	2.806	0.006
memorandum item: statistical properties of the equation	adj R^2	df	F	error probability of the entire equation	
	48.600	131	25.743	.000	

Table 13 is an invitation to consider the drivers and bottlenecks of *'smart democracy'* (see also Graph 3c of this work). The ten smartest democracies of our globe are Costa Rica; Netherlands; Jamaica; Chile; Sweden; India; Benin; Madagascar; Finland; and Germany; these are the countries of the world system, best combining democratic performance and avoiding ecological footprint. The worst performers are Sudan; Belarus; Kazakhstan; Kuwait; United Arab Emirates; Uzbekistan; Lebanon; Hong Kong, China (SAR); Azerbaijan; and Myanmar. The adjusted R^2 of our equation is 48.6%, and the F-value for the entire equation is 25.743, and the error p for the equation is .000. It is based on 132 countries with complete data. The drivers of smart democracy are feminized structures of government, economic freedom, and years of membership in the European Union. The significant bottlenecks of smart democracy are high military personnel ratios, and a high share of immigrant population. The constant of our equation is -2.037, and it is significant.

Our next Table, Table 14, analyses the drivers and bottlenecks of *'smart economic growth'* combing high economic growth with low rates of ecological footprint per capita (see also Graph 3d of this work). The IMF data for economic growth in 2010 as well as the Happy Planet Organization data on ecological footprint suggest that the 10 best performers were China; Azerbaijan; Botswana; Uzbekistan; Congo (Democratic Republic of the); Bhutan; Sudan; Mongolia; Ethiopia; and Lebanon; while the worst performers with the worst 'cocktail' of slow economic growth in relation to their ecological footprint per capita were Zimbabwe; Moldova; Lithuania; Latvia; Ukraine; Jamaica; Haiti; Armenia; Tajikistan; and Madagascar. Our equation about 'smart growth' is based on 111 countries with complete data, the R^2 is 25.2%, the F-value is 10.243, and the error probability of the entire equation is .000. The constant is 0.195, and it is not significant. Population size in relation to the global population as well as Muslim population share per total population are the significant drivers of smart development in the global system today, while absolute latitude (i.e. countries in the far North and South of the world system) as well as nations depending on worker remittances are the bottlenecks of 'smart growth' today. This again suggests, as we already hinted at in our theoretical introduction above about the theory of Andre Gunder Frank, 1999, the tectonic shifts in the geographical structures of global growth today, away from the countries of the 'North Atlantic arena' towards the nations of the Indian Ocean and the Pacific, which also thwart the smart growth efforts of the countries exporting their workforce to the hitherto existing centres of the global economy.

Table 14. Drivers and bottlenecks of smart economic growth (2010)

Independent Variable	B	Standard error	Beta	t-value	Error probability
Constant	0.195	0.178		1.092	0.277
% world population	0.099	0.031	0.261	3.149	0.002
Absolute latitude	-0.013	0.005	-0.234	-2.817	0.006
worker remittance inflows as % of GDP	-0.035	0.011	-0.262	-3.108	0.002
Muslim population share per total population	0.009	0.002	0.313	3.717	0.000
memorandum item: statistical properties of the equation	adj R^2	df	F	error probability of the entire equation	
	25.200	110	10.243	.000	

Table 15. Drivers and bottlenecks of smart gender justice

Independent Variable	B	standard error	Beta	t-value	error probability
Constant	-0.034	0.213		-0.161	0.873
% women in government. all levels	0.044	0.013	0.300	3.364	0.001
military expenditures per GDP	-0.087	0.036	-0.204	-2.403	0.018
worker remittance inflows as % of GDP	0.035	0.013	0.241	2.764	0.007
Muslim population share per total population	-0.010	0.003	-0.396	-4.153	0.000
memorandum item: statistical properties of the equation	adj R^2	df	F	error probability of the entire equation	
	39.000	92	15.712	.000	

Table 15 of our study analyses the drivers and bottlenecks of *smart gender justice.* We are comparing the given amount of gender equality in a society with the amount of resources (ecological footprint), needed to sustain it (see Graph 3e). The global best performers on this equation, how to achieve a maximum of gender justice with a minimum of ecological footprint, are the Philippines; South Africa; Finland; Norway; Mozambique; Sweden; Iceland; Kyrgyzstan; Sri Lanka; and Uganda. The worst balance sheet on this item of combing 'lilac' gender policies and 'green' issues (minimizing ecological footprint per capita) are Yemen; Saudi Arabia; United Arab Emirates; Turkey; Pakistan; Chad; Iran; Kuwait; Korea (Republic of); and Egypt. Our equation, based on the 93 countries with complete data, explains 39% of total variance, achieves an F-value of 15.712 and an error probability of the entire equation of .000. The insignificant constant has the value of -0.034. Women in government and worker remittances per GDP are the significant drivers of smart gender justice, while high military expenditures and the Muslim population share per total population are the major variables, to be interpreted as 'bottlenecks' of smart gender justice.

Table 16. Drivers and bottlenecks of smart human development

Independent Variable	B	standard error	Beta	t-value	error probability
Constant	-1.657	0.348		-4.760	0.000
% world population	0.055	0.029	0.152	1.894	0.061
public education expenditure per GNP	-0.097	0.042	-0.196	-2.283	0.024
UNDP education index	2.437	0.430	0.478	5.666	0.000
worker remittance inflows as % of GDP	0.044	0.010	0.352	4.461	0.000
memorandum item: statistical properties of the equation	adj R^2	df	F	error probability of the entire equation	
	29.900	114	13.183	.000	

Table 16 looks at the drivers and bottlenecks of *'smart human development'*. Which are the countries best combining the task of a maximum of 'human development' with a minimum of ecological footprint per capita (see also Graph 3f of this work)? The ten best practice countries on this scale are Jamaica; Philippines; Cuba; Sri Lanka; Costa Rica; Vietnam; Dominican Republic; Indonesia; Colombia; and Moldova; while all the worst performers are located in the African continent, comprising the following countries: Botswana; Namibia; Central African Rep,; Burkina Faso; Niger; Sierra Leone; Zimbabwe; Mali; Angola; and Chad. Our equation explains 29.9% of the total variance of 'smart development' and is based on the analysis of the 115 countries with complete data; the F-value is 13.183 and the error p of the entire equation is .000. The constant, which is significant, has a value of -1.657. The drivers of 'smart human development' are the share of a country's population in world population, indicating the relative size of a nation, the UNDP education index, measuring the levels of education in a given country, and worker remittance inflows as % of GDP. The bottleneck of 'smart human development' is constituted by the crowding-out effect of public education expenditures on human development.

Table 17. Drivers and bottlenecks of smart R&D

Independent Variable	B	Standard error	Beta	t-value	Error probability
Constant	0.326	0.327		0.998	0.321
Annual population growth rate. 1975-2005 (%)	-0.248	0.089	-0.253	-2.782	0.007
MNC outward investments (stock) per GDP	0.043	0.009	0.479	4.731	0.000
Openness-Index. 1990 (export-share per GDP + import-share per GDP)	-0.014	0.002	-0.552	-5.473	0.000
public education expenditure per GNP	0.136	0.051	0.235	2.646	0.010
worker remittance inflows as % of GDP	0.050	0.021	0.229	2.438	0.017
memorandum item: statistical properties of the equation	adj R^2	df	F	error probability of the entire equation	
	33.000	92	10.058	.000	

Table 17 analyses the drivers and bottlenecks of *smart R&D performance.* The equation is based on 93 countries with complete data, the R^2 is 33%, the F-value is 10.058, and the error probability of the entire equation is .000. The constant, which is not significant, is 0.326. The drivers of smart R&D performance, combining the R&D record with a minimum of ecological footprint (see also Graph 3g of this work), are the dominant position of a country on the global markets, expressed in the indicator multinational corporation outward investments per GDP, the public education expenditure, and worker remittance inflows as a % of GDP. The significant bottlenecks against a smart R&D performance are population pressure (the annual population growth rate) and world economic openness. According to our indicator, the best performing countries are the United States (because of its overwhelming performance in tertiary education and research, its high ecological footprint notwithstanding); Sweden; New Zealand; Finland; Israel; United Kingdom; Netherlands; Norway; Switzerland; and Kyrgyzstan. The worst performers are: United Arab Emirates; Luxembourg; Kuwait; Namibia; Botswana; Cyprus; Bosnia and Herzegovina; Macedonia; Uruguay; and the Czech Republic.

Our last result is presented in Table 18. It features on the preconditions of *'smart social cohesion',* combining a relatively high social cohesion with a relatively low ecological footprint (see also Graph 3h). Our equation is based on an analysis of 120 countries with complete data, the adjusted R^2 is just 8.7%, and the F-value is 6.771; and the error probability of the entire equation is .002. The constant is 0.824 and is significant. There are two significant bottlenecks and no positive drivers of smart social cohesion – annual population growth (population pressure) and the crowding-out effects of public education expenditures per GDP. The best results on our indicator are achieved by several less developed and or (former) communist or left wing regime countries as well as nations with a known record of relatively egalitarian development policies (South Korea), with the entire group comprising: Chad; Uzbekistan; Rwanda; Belarus; Laos; Cuba; Benin; Tajikistan; Korea (Republic of); and Thailand. The worst record of combing social cohesion with low ecological footprints was found in Djibouti; Namibia; Bosnia and Herzegovina; Central African Republic; Sierra Leone; Botswana; Macedonia; Bolivia; South Africa; and Colombia.

Table 18. Drivers and bottlenecks of smart social cohesion

Independent Variable	B	Standard error	Beta	t-value	Error probability
Constant	0.824	0.206		4.009	0.000
Annual population growth rate. 1975-2005 (%)	-0.152	0.055	-0.248	-2.775	0.006
public education expenditure per GNP	-0.102	0.034	-0.270	-3.013	0.003
memorandum item: statistical properties of the equation	adj R^2	df	F	error probability of the entire equation	
	8.700	119	6.771	.002	

Chapter 4

DISCUSSION OF THE RESULTS SO FAR

Knight and Rosa, 2011 compared the ecological footprint per capita and average life satisfaction (as a measure of subjective well-being). Based on maximum likelihood estimations, they tested the effects of climate, political, economic, and social factors on EWEB with a sample of 105 countries. Knight and Rosa found a negative quadratic effect of economic development on EWEB, a negative effect of income inequality, and a positive effect of social capital (based on social trust data, contained in the *World Values Survey)*[32].

Our residuals-based reformulation of smart development realistically captures the trade-off between Global Ecological Footprint per capita and development performance and offers to us a better idea about smart development performance at different stages of socio-economic development. Our results show that traditional indicators of economic globalization and also inequality have little influence on smart development performance, but that hitherto neglected elements of dependency and world systems theory gain in importance. This is especially relevant for the socio-economic theory of Samir Amin, but it is also true of the contributions by feminism, peace research, and by other various approaches in the globalization critical tradition, perhaps hitherto neglected here and there, and

---

[32] http://www.worldvaluessurvey.org/

now summarized in Table 9 of this work. Efficiency tends to increase and then to decrease with rising development levels. Big countries with large population resources perform better on our scales, and military expenditures/personnel rates are a significant block against smart development performance. In a sense, our results also contradict the logic inherent in the 'beautiful', but unfortunately wrong *'small is beautiful'* analysis, proposed by Schumacher, 1973a: not the small countries, but the big countries find it easier to have a satisfactory smart development performance in comparison to the ecological footprint, consumed by them. Our research also shows the beneficial effects of migration on the sending countries. Worker remittances have a significant positive effect on the HPI and a host of other smart development indicators. Migration sending countries, as to be expected from Samir Amin's dependency theory, reap substantial benefits from receiving worker remittances, while other indicators of globalization hardly affect the smart development performance. Table 19 now shows the significant standardized regression coefficients, as they emerged from Tables 10 – 18 of this work, again linked to the theories presented in this work:

Table 19. Testing of the theories

Independent Variable	Dependent variable	Beta
Feminism: % women in government, all levels (feminist theory, stressing the need to feminize structures of government)	overall smart development index, based on 26 variables, weighted equally	0,185
	Smart democracy	0,196
	Smart gender justice	0,300
% world population (Amin's five monopolies of power)	Smart human development	0,152
	Happy Life Years	0,161
	Smart economic growth	0,261
2000 Economic Freedom Score (its absence is explained either by Amin's critique of rent-seeking seeking in the periphery versus conventional neo-liberal theories of economic growth)	overall smart development index, based on 26 variables, weighted equally	0,336

Independent Variable	Dependent variable	Beta
	overall smart development index, based on 26 variables, weighting equally the six component dimensions	0,402
	Smart democracy	0,457
Absolute latitude (Andre Gunder Frank's 'Re-Orient' model)	Smart economic growth	-0,234
Annual population growth rate, 1975-2005 (%) (Paul Israel Singer's dependency theory)	Smart R&D	-0,253
	Smart social cohesion	-0,248
Immigration - Share of population 2005 (%) (Amin's theory about the role of migration)	Smart democracy	-0,348
military expenditures per GDP (quantitative dependency and peace research approaches)	Happy Life Years	-0,245
	Smart gender justice	-0,204
	overall smart development index, based on 26 variables, weighted equally	-0,191
	overall smart development index, based on 26 variables, weighting equally the six component dimensions	-0,166
military personnel rate ln (quantitative dependency and peace research approaches)	Smart democracy	-0,221
MNC outward investments (stock) per GDP (Bornschier's dependency theory, stressing the importance of MNC headquarter status in international society)	Smart R&D	0,479
Muslim population share per total population (Amin's critique of Islamism, implicitly expecting a negative trade-off with development performance versus Andre Gunder Frank's 'Re-Orient' model, expecting a transfer of growth and productive activities to the global East and South)	Smart gender justice	-0,396
	Smart economic growth	0,313
Openness-Index, 1990 (export-share per GDP + import-share per GDP) (Amin's conception of the role of the peripheries)	Smart R&D	-0,552

Table 19. (Continued).

Independent Variable	Dependent variable	Beta
	overall smart development index, based on 26 variables, weighting equally the six component dimensions	-0,222
	overall smart development index, based on 26 variables, weighted equally	-0,170
population density (José Carlos Mariategui's dependency theory)	overall smart development index, based on 26 variables, weighted equally	0,214
public education expenditure per GNP (human capital approaches in the tradition of the UNDP versus Kalecki/Steindl paradigm versus neo-liberal approaches, featuring a 'crowding out' phenomenon)	Smart social cohesion	-0,270
	Smart human development	-0,196
	Smart R&D	0,235
UNDP education index (human capital approaches in the tradition of the UNDP versus Kalecki/Steindl paradigm)	overall smart development index, based on 26 variables, weighted equally	0,198
	Smart human development	0,478
worker remittance inflows as % of GDP (conventional centre-periphery models about the negative consequences of the brain drain versus 'new migration theories', underlining the positive effects of worker remittances on migration sending countries)	Smart economic growth	-0,262
	overall smart development index, based on 26 variables, weighting equally the six component dimensions	0,177
	overall smart development index, based on 26 variables, weighted equally	0,208
	Smart R&D	0,229
	Smart gender justice	0,241
	Happy Life Years	0,288
	Smart human development	0,352
Years of membership in the EU, 2010 (Amin's theory about the importance of European integration as a counterweight to US dominance in the world system)	Smart democracy	0,183

Only the following significant effects highlight the necessity to further develop the paradigm, developed here: the negative, crowding out effects public education expenditures per GDP on smart social cohesion and smart human development, and the negative effects, worker remittance inflows as % of GDP wield on smart economic growth. The impressive list of tests, speaking in favour of the globalization critical paradigm, presented in this work, would suggest to further developing this research approach to questions of 'smart development'.

First of all, the *dependency and world systems paradigm by Samir Amin* comes to my mind. As correctly predicted by Samir Amin, the big countries with huge population resources today are favoured in their smart economic growth, their Happy Life Years, and their smart human development. As correctly expected by Amin, peripheral rent seeking is a burden and its absence, measured by economic freedom, is an asset among the forces, shaping international development today, especially for smart democracy, and the overall smart development index (both formulations, used in this essay). In addition, Amin correctly stresses the necessity for European integration – and the positive effects of years of EU membership on smart democracy confirm is Euro-optimism. He correctly analyses the enormous transfer of resources from the centre to the periphery, brought about by migration, with the huge statistical observed effects of received worker remittances on smart human development, Happy Life Years, smart gender justice, smart R&D, and both formulations of the smart development index justifying his assumption. Amin's dependency theory correctly predicts the very negative effects of world economic openness on smart development. The huge statistical negative and very uniform effects, to be observed, cannot be simply and easily rejected out of hand: smart R&D and overall smart development (both formulations) are affected negatively by world economic openness. Among the major four founding figures of the 'world systems approach' (Amin, Arrighi, Frank and Wallerstein, 1982) he is the only one to have come up, in addition, with a consistent and far-reaching critique of Islamism, confirmed by the very negative trade-off between Muslim population share and smart gender empowerment.

But in some ways, Amin's paradigm has to be expanded and refined: *Feminism* is an important driver of smart gender justice, smart democracy, and the overall smart development index, based on 26 variables, weighted equally. Feminist approaches, in principle, would be well compatible with Amin's original approach. The *Kalecki/Steindl paradigm* also can be merged with Amin's theory, and it has three significant results to its favour – the positive determination of smart R&D by public education expenditures, and the positive effects of the UNDP education index on smart human development and on overall smart development index, based on 26 variables, weighted equally. Several further strains of dependency/world systems research are confirmed in this essay: *Bornschier's dependency theory* and the importance it attaches to multinational corporation headquarter status, which is confirmed by the positive effect of this variable on smart R&D; and the effect of population density, predicted in *José Carlos Mariategui's dependency theory* on the overall smart development index, based on 26 variables, weighted equally. *Paul Israel Singer's approach to dependency and population dynamics* is confirmed by the significant negative effects of annual population growth rates on smart R&D and smart social cohesion. The following empirical results could be interpreted to be expressions of *Andre Gunder Frank's Re-Orient hypothesis,* 1999 about a fundamental shift in the global production dynamics away from the old centres towards the countries of the Indian and the Pacific Ocean: the significant positive effect of Muslim population share per total population on smart economic growth, and the significant negative effects of absolute latitude on smart economic growth, of immigration - share of population in 2005 on smart democracy (the biggest migration recipients are the countries of the global 'North'), and worker remittance inflows as % of GDP on smart economic growth.

For some other processes, the empirical Amin's five monopolies of power include two elements of military might, the monopoly of technology, supported by military expenditures of the dominant nations, and the monopoly of the military means of mass destruction. But the significant negative effects of military expenditures (on Happy Life Years, smart gender justice, the two formulations of the overall smart development index) or military personnel rates (smart democracy) on smart development rather support the arguments of *quantitative peace research* during the last decades with its apprehensions against very high military spending rates (Auvinen and Nafziger, 1999; Heo, 1998; Mintz and Stevenson, 1995).

As we stated, the real differences with the theories presented here are to be found in the negative effects of public education expenditures on *public education expenditures per GDP* on smart social cohesion and smart human development. In this case, our response can only be to draw the global research community to the essays published by *Blankenau and Simpson,* 2004 and *Sylwester,* 2000, written from the perspective of established economic theory. Blankenau and Simpson, 2004, because, as we already stated, they investigated the public education expenditure-growth relationship in the context of an endogenous growth model in which private and public investment are inputs to human capital accumulation. They could show that the positive direct effect of public education spending on growth can be diminished or even negated when other determinants of growth are negatively affected by general equilibrium adjustments. Blankenau and Simpson showed that the response of growth to public education expenditures may be nonmonotonic. The relationship depends on the level of government spending, the tax structure and the parameters of production technologies. Sylwester, 2000, for his part could demonstrate that although public education expenditures are positively associated with future economic growth, the contemporaneous effect upon growth is negative.

Chapter 5

INEQUALITY AND SMART PUBLIC HEALTH DEVELOPMENT

In the following, we take up a very hotly debated issue, which has been very prominent in recent global public health debate. Following the path-breaking articles by RG Wilkinson, 1992, 1997; and Wilkinson and Picket, 2006, income inequality has a very detrimental effect on life quality. But life quality also depends in a non-linear fashion from environmental data. Already in Graph 2 above we portrayed this trade-off, stating that the non-linear tradeoffs between *'energy consumption and/or environmental strain'* and *'life quality'* were first portrayed in Goldstein, 1985. We already hinted at the fact that social science literature widely uses non-linear functions to depict the trade-off (see Afxentiou, 1990a, 1990b; Anand and Ravillion, 1993; Anson, 1988, 1991; Cheng, 1989; Dixon, 1987; Dixon and Moon, 1986, 1989; Fosu, 2009, 2010a, 2010b, 2010c; Kakwani, 1993, 1995; Khan, 1991; King, 1998; Knight and Rosa, 2011; Mazumdar, 1996, 2000; Moon and Dixon, 1992; Newman and Thomson, 1989; Rudra, 2009; Tausch and Prager, 1993). Following the public health debate contribution in Tausch,

2010 and the social scientific approaches in Fain, et al. 1997; Mostafa, 2010a and 2010b; Mostafa and Nataraajan, 2009; Shandra, 2007a, 2007b, Shandra, Leckband, McKinney and London, 2009, we now portray in Graph 4a-4c the trade-off between ecological footprint and life quality.

Table 20 portrays the mathematical properties of this trade-off:

Table 20. The trade-off between ecological footprint and life quality

life quality indicator (dependent variable)	Independent variables	Regression coefficient B	Standard error	Beta	T	Error probability
life expectancy	Constant	51,057	1,802		28,330	0,000
	footprint per capita	8,493	1,054	1,623	8,061	0,000
	footprint per capita^2	-0,609	0,118	-1,041	-5,173	0,000
	statistical parameters of the equation	adj R^2	0.488			
		n =	140,000			
		F =	67,222			
		error p =	.000			
female survival	Constant	45,541	3,091		14,735	0,000
	footprint per capita	14,346	1,810	1,643	7,926	0,000
	footprint per capita^2	-1,065	0,202	-1,091	-5,263	0,000
	statistical parameters of the equation	adj R^2	0.463			
		n =	139,000			
		F =	60,508			
		error p =	.000			
infant mortality	Constant	100,458	6,395		15,709	0,000
	footprint per capita	-31,745	3,752	-1,721	-8,461	0,000
	footprint per capita^2	2,401	0,418	1,167	5,740	0,000
	statistical parameters of the equation	adj R^2	0.485			
		n =	138,000			
		F =	65,634			
		error p =	.000			

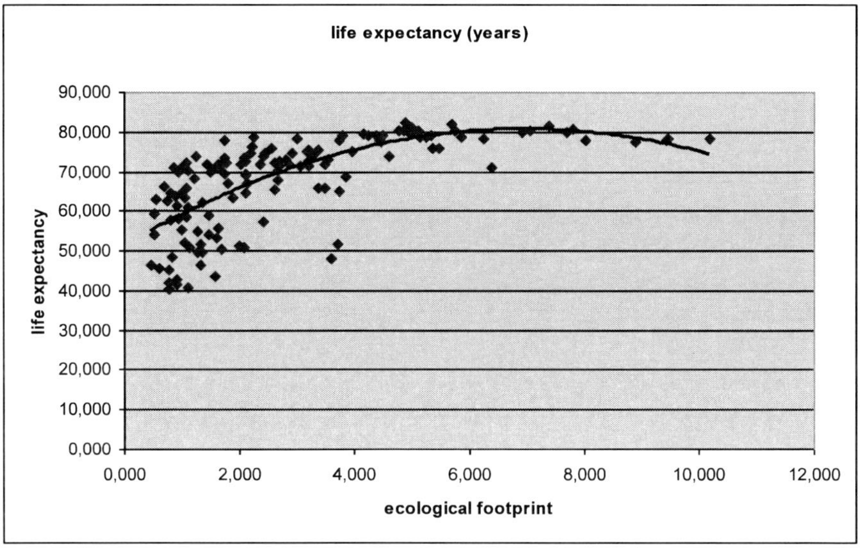

Graph 4a. Life expectancy and ecological footprint.

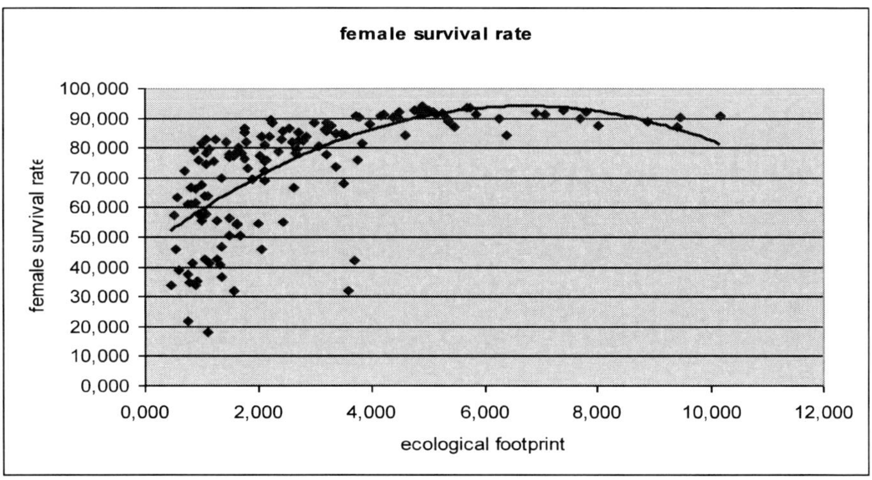

Graph 4b. Female survival rate and ecological footprint.

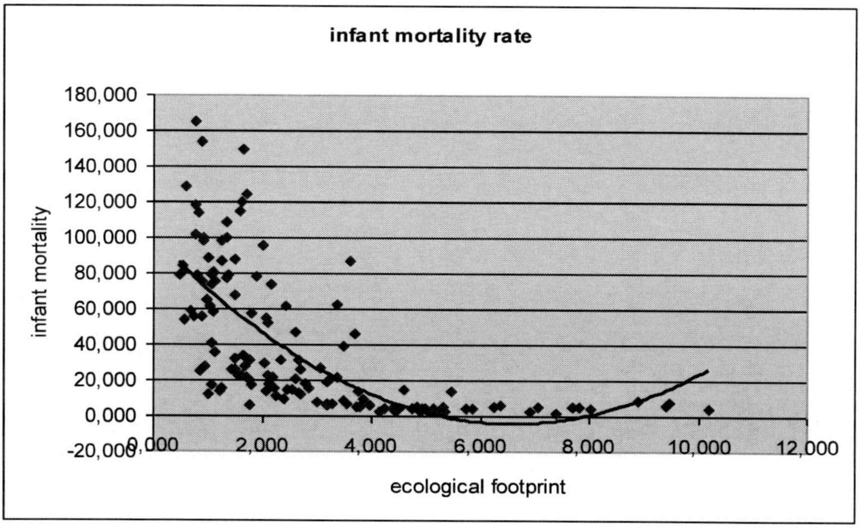

Graph 4c. Female survival rate and ecological footprint.

Table 21. Explaining the z-standardized residuals from ecological footprint and life expectancy (ecologically efficient life expectancy; smart life expectancy)

	Regression coefficient B	Standard error	Beta	T	Error probability
Constant	-1,305	0,521		-2,503	0,014
Membership in the Islamic Conference	-1,606	0,598	-0,735	-2,686	0,009
military expenditures per GDP	-0,084	0,039	-0,194	-2,125	0,037
public education expenditure per GNP	-0,124	0,049	-0,244	-2,554	0,013
UNDP education index	2,529	0,568	0,483	4,450	0,000
worker remittance inflows as % of GDP	0,039	0,014	0,263	2,811	0,006
Muslim population share per total population	0,025	0,007	0,960	3,367	0,001
quintile share income difference between richest and poorest 20%	-0,018	0,010	-0,156	-1,710	0,091

adj. R^2 = 0.364; n = 88; F = 8.108; error p = .000

Our calculations show that inequality, as correctly predicted by R. G. Wilkinson and his school of public health research, has a detrimental effect on life expectancy (smart life expectancy) and on female survival (smart female survival), but that the effect on smart infant mortality reduction does not materialize, once we properly control for the other intervening variables. Let us look first at the statistical results of our research, given in Table 21.

Table 22. Explaining the z-standardized residuals from ecological footprint and female survival rate (ecologically efficient female survival rate, smart female survival)

	Regression coefficient B	Standard error	Beta	T	Error probability
Constant	-1,289	0,512		-2,519	0,014
Membership in the Islamic Conference	-1,573	0,587	-0,714	-2,679	0,009
military expenditures per GDP	-0,075	0,039	-0,174	-1,953	0,054
public education expenditure per GNP	-0,141	0,048	-0,276	-2,960	0,004
UNDP education index	2,582	0,558	0,490	4,627	0,000
worker remittance inflows as % of GDP	0,036	0,014	0,237	2,599	0,011
Muslim population share per total population	0,026	0,007	0,999	3,596	0,001
quintile share income difference between richest and poorest 20%	-0,022	0,010	-0,187	-2,114	0,038

adj. R^2 = 0.396; n = 88; F = 9.157; error p = .000

The *significant negative results of inequality* on the female survival rate (ecologically efficient female survival rate, smart female survival, beta weight -0,187) and on life expectancy (ecologically efficient life expectancy; smart life expectancy, beta weight -0,156) have to be re-iterated. However, we must also observe that *Membership in the Organization of Islamic Cooperation* has a significant negative effect on life expectancy (ecologically efficient life expectancy; smart life expectancy) and on the female survival rate (ecologically efficient female survival rate, smart female survival). This results reflects the existing deficiencies of 'real existing' Muslim countries in the world today, while Muslim societies as such *(share of Muslim population per total population)* have a significant and positive effect on life expectancy (ecologically efficient life expectancy; smart life expectancy) and on the female survival rate (ecologically efficient female survival rate, smart female survival).

Table 23. Explaining the z-standardized residuals from ecological footprint and infant mortality

	Regression coefficient B	Standard error	Beta	T	Error probability
Constant	1,420	0,498		2,851	0,006
Membership in the Islamic Conference	0,863	0,571	0,444	1,511	0,135
military expenditures per GDP	0,044	0,038	0,116	1,180	0,241
public education expenditure per GNP	0,080	0,046	0,177	1,724	0,089
UNDP education index	-2,266	0,543	-0,487	-4,175	0,000
worker remittance inflows as % of GDP	-0,043	0,013	-0,327	-3,255	0,002
Muslim population share per total population	-0,012	0,007	-0,506	-1,653	0,102
quintile share income difference between richest and poorest 20%	0,004	0,010	0,036	0,369	0,713

adj. R^2 = 0.267; n = 88; F = 5.522; error p = .000

The effects of *public education expenditure rates* again confirm their crowding-out effects on life quality, already described in this work (beta weights):

female survival rate (ecologically efficient female survival rate, smart female survival)	-0,276
life expectancy (ecologically efficient life expectancy; smart life expectancy)	-0,244
infant mortality considering ecological footprint	0,177

Similar crowding-out effects are to be observed for *military expenditures per GDP*:

life expectancy (ecologically efficient life expectancy; smart life expectancy)	-0,194
female survival rate (ecologically efficient female survival rate, smart female survival)	-0,174

The *UNDP education index*, as to be expected from the other results of this work, has the following very beneficial significant beta-weights on our smart development indicators:

life expectancy (ecologically efficient life expectancy; smart life expectancy)	0,483
female survival rate (ecologically efficient female survival rate, smart female survival)	0,490
infant mortality considering ecological footprint	-0,487

Last, but not least, the effects of *worker remittances per GDP* are the following:

infant mortality considering ecological footprint	-0,327
life expectancy (ecologically efficient life expectancy; smart life expectancy)	0,263
female survival rate (ecologically efficient female survival rate, smart female survival)	0,237

Thus, the Wilkinson research agenda finds its proper place also in debates about ‘smart development’, but certainly, the weight of other variables, such as

- Membership in the Islamic Conference
- military expenditures per GDP
- Muslim population share per total population
- public education expenditure per GNP
- UNDP education index
- worker remittance inflows as % of GDP

also has to be properly taken into account.

Conclusion

Since all existing major comparative empirical studies on drivers and bottlenecks of environmental quality only touched upon different dependent variables, and not the smart development, this our first international comparative study seems to suggest cautiously that future research efforts in comparative environmental science would be well advised to take the major predictor variables of the present study as well as the environmental plateau curve into account (see also Weede and Kampf, 2002; de Haan, Lundstrom and Sturm, 2006; and Gwartney, Lawson and Holcombe, 1999).

It emerges that the absence of 'rent seeking', *economic freedom* and a free price mechanism, and *worker remittances* are the most important drivers of 'smart development'. Most of the *'small is beautiful'* assumptions of *Schumacherian economics* by contrast do not stand the test of cross-national development accounting and are *squarely contradicted* by our empirical results; with population density and population size always being among the drivers, and not the bottlenecks of 'smart development'.

As correctly predicted by Samir Amin, the *big countries with huge population resources* today are favoured in their smart economic growth, their Happy Life Years, and their smart human development. As correctly expected by Amin, peripheral rent seeking is a burden and its absence, measured by economic freedom, is an asset among the forces, shaping international development today, especially for smart democracy, and the overall smart development index (both formulations, used in this essay). In addition, Amin correctly stressed the necessity for *European integration* – and the positive effects of years of EU membership on smart democracy confirm is Euro-optimism. He correctly analysed the enormous transfer of resources from the centre to the periphery, brought about by *migration*, with the huge statistical observed effects of received worker remittances on smart human development, Happy Life Years, smart gender justice, smart R&D, and both formulations of the smart development index justifying his assumption. Amin's dependency theory correctly predicted the *very negative effects of world economic openness on smart development*. The huge statistical negative and very uniform effects, to be observed, cannot be simply easily rejected out of hand: smart R&D, and overall smart development (both formulations) are affected negatively by world economic openness. Among the major four founding figures of the 'world systems approach' (Amin, Arrighi, Frank and Wallerstein, 1982) he is the only one to have come up, in addition, with a consistent and far-reaching critique of *Islamism*, confirmed by the very negative trade-off between Muslim population share and smart gender empowerment.

We could also show in this book the importance of Feminism, the Kalecki/Steindl paradigm, the multinational corporation headquarter status, population density, population dynamics, Muslim population share per total population, absolute latitude, and migration on 'smart development'. We also investigated the negative effects of public education expenditures on public education expenditures per GDP on smart development.

We are aware that our answers, raised to the questions in this book, are incomplete. But we hope to have provided at least some preliminary guiding posts for further research on this important subject.

APPENDIX

Appendix Table 1. The dependent variables

democracy	1	Combined Failed States Index
democracy	2	Civil and Political Liberties violations
democracy	3	Corruption avoidance measure
democracy	4	Democracy measure
democracy	5	Global tolerance index
democracy	6	Rule of law
economic growth	7	Crisis Performance Factor
economic growth	8	economic growth IMF prediction growth rate in 2009
economic growth	9	economic growth IMF prediction growth rate in 2010
economic growth	10	economic growth in real terms pc. per annum, 1990-2005
gender	11	closing economic gender gap
gender	12	closing educational gender gap
gender	13	closing health and survivial gender gap
gender	14	closing of global gender gap overall score 2009
gender	15	closing political gender gap
gender	16	gender empowerment index value
human development	17	Infant mortality 2005
human development	18	female survival probability of surviving to age 65 female
human development	19	Human development index (HDI) value 2004
human development	20	Life Expectancy (years)
human development	21	Life Satisfaction (0-10)
R&D	22	Country share in top world 500 Universities
R&D	23	per capita world class universities
R&D	24	tertiary enrollment
social cohesion	25	quintile share income difference between richest and poorest 20%
social cohesion	26	unemployment rate

Appendix Table 1. (Continued).

nonparametric_26 equal weights	27	overall 26 development index
nonparametric, weighting each dimension equally	28	overall 26 development index, based on six dimensions
	29	component UNDP-type index for overall democracy-performance
	30	component UNDP-type index for overall economic growth-performance
	31	component UNDP-type index for overall gender-performance
	32	component UNDP-type index for overall human development-performance
	33	component UNDP-type index for overall R&D-performance
	34	component UNDP-type index for overall social cohesion-performance
	35	% women in government, all levels
	36	% world population
	37	2000 Economic Freedom Score
	38	Absolute latitude
	39	Annual population growth rate, 1975-2005 (%)
	40	comparative price levels (US=1.00)
	41	foreign savings rate
	42	FPZ (free production zones) employment as % of total population
	43	ln GDP per capita
	44	ln GDP per capita ^2
	45	Membership in the Islamic Conference
	46	military expenditures per GDP
	47	military personnel rate ln (MPR+1)
	48	MNC outward investments (stock) per GDP
	49	MNC PEN - stock of Inward FDI per GDP
	50	MNC PEN: DYN MNC PEN 1995-2005
	51	Openness-Index, 1990 (export-share per GDP + import-share per GDP)
	52	population density
	53	public education expenditure per GNP
	54	UNDP education index
	55	worker remittance inflows as % of GDP
	56	Immigration - Share of population 2005 (%)
	57	Muslim population share per total population
	58	net international migration rate, 2005-2010
	59	Years of membership in the EU, 2010
	60	years of membership in EMU, 2010
	61	social security expenditure per GDP average 1990s (ILO)
	62	ecological footprint (g ha/cap)
	63	ecological footprint (g ha/cap)^2

Appendix Table 2. Global smart development

	z_res_overall 26 development index	z_res_overall 26 development index, based on six dimensions	z_res_component UNDP democracy	z_res_component UNDP economic growth	z_res_component UNDP gender	z_res_component UNDP human development	z_res_component UNDP R&D	z_res_component UNDP social cohesion
Sudan	-2,512	-3,117	-2,788	1,650		-1,516	-0,941	
Bosnia and Herzegovina	-2,381	-2,858	-1,304	-1,251		-0,270	-1,536	-3,805
Kuwait	-1,887	-2,552	-2,290	0,693	-1,717	-0,328	-2,514	
Djibouti	-0,705	-2,500	0,185	0,478		-0,853	-0,437	-5,940
Namibia	-1,185	-2,428	-0,260	0,362	-0,013	-2,457	-1,797	-4,061
Central African Republic,	-2,214	-2,410	-0,565	-0,190		-2,382	-0,480	-2,692
Macedonia	-1,396	-1,853	-1,499	0,047	-0,839	-0,760	-1,529	-2,020
Togo	-0,979	-1,830	0,075	-1,201		-0,423	0,255	
Congo (Democratic Republic)	-0,850	-1,756	-0,657	1,822		-1,249	0,315	
Lebanon	-1,299	-1,731	-1,842	1,470		-0,339	0,015	
United Arab Emirates	-1,970	-1,725	-2,260	0,211	-2,158	-0,003	-2,816	-0,310
Botswana	-1,075	-1,684	0,524	2,091	-0,787	-3,052	-1,789	-2,127
Sierra Leone	-1,400	-1,617	0,271	0,007		-2,032	0,241	-2,645
Angola	-0,669	-1,543	-0,511	0,053	0,423	-1,811	0,057	
Congo	-0,481	-1,488	0,125	-0,376		-0,242	0,380	
Zimbabwe	-1,750	-1,264	-1,035	-2,819	-0,314	-1,956	-0,004	0,268
Niger	-1,888	-1,257	-0,500	0,306		-2,104	-0,537	-0,029
Chad	-1,827	-1,084	-1,350	0,144	-1,876	-1,749	-0,614	1,071
Estonia	-1,303	-0,972	-0,788	-0,956	-0,319	-1,091	-0,850	0,258
Turkey	-1,134	-0,946	-0,744	-0,902	-2,091	0,100	-0,729	-0,004
Iran	-1,021	-0,934	-1,376	1,002	-1,785	-0,012	-1,341	-0,111
Hong Kong, China (SAR)	-1,528	-0,921	-1,728	0,077		-0,106	-0,400	0,236
Kazakhstan	-1,327	-0,882	-2,334	0,008	0,365	-0,797	-0,614	0,384
Paraguay	-0,519	-0,849	-1,164	0,016	0,195	-0,014	-1,339	-0,894
Burkina Faso	-1,312	-0,817	-0,556	0,784	-1,033	-2,120	-0,850	0,800
Mauritania	-0,643	-0,758	-0,737	0,513	-0,557	-0,733	-0,663	-0,782
Saudi Arabia	-1,064	-0,701	-1,522	-0,096	-2,211	0,718	-0,443	0,271
Cameroon	-1,097	-0,699	-1,098	-0,343	-0,571	-1,220	-0,095	0,221

Appendix Table 2. (Continued).

	z_res_overall 26 development index	z_res_overall 26 development index, based on six dimensions	z_res_component UNDP democracy	z_res_component UNDP economic growth	z_res_component UNDP gender	z_res_component UNDP human development	z_res_component UNDP R&D	z_res_component UNDP social cohesion
Russia	-1,324	-0,681	-1,631	-1,070	-0,230	-0,645	0,546	0,399
Haiti	-0,765	-0,632	-0,423	-1,672		0,349	0,388	-0,970
Burundi	-1,598	-0,624	-0,360	-0,660		-1,480	0,142	0,738
Nigeria	-1,092	-0,610	-0,907	-0,198	-0,341	-1,463	-0,181	0,430
Uruguay	-0,508	-0,591	-0,227	1,197	-0,628	-0,574	-1,420	-0,176
Mali	-0,687	-0,559	0,751	0,724	-1,239	-1,889	-0,508	-0,127
Guinea	-1,292	-0,557	-0,553	0,120		-1,047	-0,243	0,603
Belarus	-1,445	-0,537	-2,546	-0,141	0,419	-0,489	0,097	0,960
Greece	-0,612	-0,494	-0,430	0,604	-0,904	-0,273	-0,834	0,113
Syria	-0,427	-0,494	-1,629	0,454	-0,790	0,798	-0,705	-0,384
Czech Republic	-0,564	-0,485	-0,195	0,019	-0,643	-0,337	-1,381	0,602
Malta	-0,404	-0,401	-0,643	0,267	-0,868	0,470	-1,227	0,234
Singapore	-0,643	-0,401	-0,722	-1,257	-1,033	0,386	0,131	0,399
Luxembourg	-0,010	-0,394	0,308	-0,634	0,016	0,713	-2,801	-0,709
Yemen	-0,705	-0,356	-0,401	0,943	-2,996	0,145	0,038	0,020
Mexico	-0,288	-0,297	-0,358	-0,468	-0,564	0,407	-0,983	0,322
Korea (Republic of)	-0,390	-0,293	-0,157	0,164	-1,589	0,376	-1,217	0,833
Azerbaijan	-0,923	-0,260	-1,699	2,893	-1,237	-0,152	-0,129	-0,057
Venezuela	-0,302	-0,240	-0,720	-1,194	0,023	0,484	-0,349	0,155
Ukraine	-0,571	-0,213	-0,542	-2,114	-0,004	0,043	0,314	0,579
Bolivia	0,200	-0,201	0,273	0,332	-0,293	0,037	0,431	-1,748
Ethiopia	-0,626	-0,198	-0,120	1,498	-0,950	-1,593	-0,297	0,701
Cyprus	-0,122	-0,191	0,314	1,022	-1,037	0,214	-1,654	0,345
Egypt	-0,294	-0,158	-0,946	0,463	-1,556	1,053	-0,609	0,174
Mongolia	-0,051	-0,150	0,373	1,579	0,022	-1,043	-0,594	-0,337
Myanmar	-0,799	-0,150	-1,636	1,165		0,274	0,305	0,228
Rwanda	-1,105	-0,129	-0,270	0,548		-1,277	0,202	1,012
Zambia	-0,226	-0,110	0,731	-0,100	-0,162	-1,545	0,254	-0,228
Algeria	-0,151	-0,098	-0,941	0,245	-0,643	0,840	-0,028	-0,461
Albania	0,172	-0,074	-0,216	0,404	-0,661	0,870	-0,465	-0,724
Belize	0,466	-0,052	0,301	0,296	-0,222	0,732	-1,286	-0,543
Guyana	0,372	-0,033	0,100	1,092	0,854	-0,297	-0,967	-0,707
South Africa	0,682	-0,013	1,216	-0,472	2,001	-1,156	-0,086	-1,625

	z_res_overall 26 development index	z_res_overall 26 development index, based on six dimensions	z_res_component UNDP democracy	z_res_component UNDP economic growth	z_res_component UNDP gender	z_res_component UNDP human development	z_res_component UNDP R&D	z_res_component UNDP social cohesion
Kenya	-0,287	-0,009	-0,220	-0,158	0,245	-0,966	0,006	0,473
Romania	-0,091	0,009	0,012	-1,035	-0,143	0,274	-0,436	0,607
Croatia	0,105	0,050	-0,057	-0,553	0,128	0,480	-0,614	0,279
Ecuador	0,597	0,055	-0,065	-0,886	0,833	0,874	-1,027	-0,363
Latvia	-0,218	0,069	0,132	-2,330	0,740	-0,094	0,585	0,464
Brazil	0,547	0,076	0,432	-0,351	-0,061	0,783	-0,342	-0,860
Portugal	0,183	0,135	0,926	-0,428	-0,197	-0,088	-0,175	0,162
Pakistan	-0,224	0,146	0,154	-0,359	-2,079	0,567	0,118	0,669
Italy	-0,010	0,183	0,262	-0,481	-0,658	0,173	0,714	0,392
Uganda	-0,127	0,204	-0,740	1,444	1,261	-1,262	-0,261	0,598
Malaysia	0,099	0,205	0,031	-0,596	-0,679	0,853	-0,088	0,365
Laos	-0,435	0,209	-1,066	0,788		0,519	-0,091	0,939
Armenia	0,034	0,216	0,095	-1,643	-0,964	1,129	0,362	0,253
Lithuania	0,059	0,224	0,564	-2,577	0,517	0,229	0,343	0,670
Slovakia	0,332	0,226	0,432	0,161	-0,037	0,312	-0,587	0,247
Spain	0,204	0,240	0,323	0,058	0,226	0,029	0,130	0,143
Iceland	0,389	0,248	0,837	-1,138	1,598	0,024	-1,379	0,392
Uzbekistan	0,046	0,310	-1,931	1,830	0,796	0,315	-0,727	1,055
Tanzania	0,222	0,311	0,508	0,890	0,606	-1,455	-0,153	0,592
Colombia	0,880	0,347	0,058	-0,755	0,612	1,404	0,198	-1,137
Poland	0,233	0,349	0,255	0,733	-0,040	0,058	0,236	0,191
Benin	0,010	0,351	1,383	-0,079	-1,054	-0,921	0,081	0,896
Ireland	0,417	0,381	0,618	-0,794	0,489	-0,044	0,564	0,333
Japan	0,104	0,384	0,889	-0,609	-0,705	0,193	0,462	0,744
Panama	0,765	0,396	0,492	1,456	0,194	0,555	-0,346	-0,720
Cambodia	0,228	0,398	0,045	-0,337	0,067	-0,117	0,109	0,752
Slovenia	0,174	0,410	0,606	0,430	-0,392	0,138	-0,018	0,671
Hungary	0,280	0,410	0,986	-0,467	-0,172	0,015	0,137	0,575
Bulgaria	0,375	0,422	0,376	-0,981	0,498	0,398	0,201	0,397
Jordan	0,232	0,425	-0,467	0,519	-0,558	1,033	0,474	-0,023
Ghana	0,559	0,437	1,006	0,865	0,285	-0,560	-0,342	0,033
Guatemala	0,694	0,471	0,392	-0,538	-0,123	1,204	-0,154	-0,171
Tunisia	0,584	0,497	-0,027	0,798	-0,555	1,143	0,156	-0,249
Israel	0,218	0,528	-0,155	0,204	-0,416	0,135	2,179	0,211
Senegal	0,476	0,537	1,064	0,113	0,099	-0,378	-0,219	0,581
Honduras	0,847	0,577	0,376	-0,359	0,604	0,866	-0,128	-0,040

Appendix Table 2. (Continued).

	z_res_overall 26 development index	z_res_overall 26 development index, based on six dimensions	z_res_component UNDP democracy	z_res_component UNDP economic growth	z_res_component UNDP gender	z_res_component UNDP human development	z_res_component UNDP R&D	z_res_component UNDP social cohesion
Madagascar	0,638	0,595	1,378	-1,269	1,024	-0,445	-0,038	0,412
Georgia	0,433	0,602	0,207	-0,708	-0,702	1,162	1,240	-0,226
Nicaragua	0,728	0,611	0,338	-0,396	0,850	0,756	-0,471	0,433
China	0,438	0,626	-1,255	3,239	-0,380	0,893	-0,093	0,391
Morocco	0,581	0,632	0,119	0,450	-0,688	1,164	0,238	0,093
Nepal	0,689	0,649	0,922	-0,174	-0,539	0,583	0,344	0,026
France	0,650	0,662	0,812	0,060	0,492	0,132	0,711	0,271
El Salvador	1,137	0,681	0,834	-0,908	0,751	1,180	0,108	-0,531
Canada	0,610	0,682	0,682	0,632	0,179	-0,066	1,140	0,109
Australia	0,598	0,698	0,542	0,689	0,276	0,025	1,080	0,013
Belgium	0,692	0,730	0,793	-0,063	0,369	0,119	1,217	0,293
Mozambique	0,591	0,737	0,934	0,580	1,791	-1,545	0,032	0,732
Argentina	0,998	0,764	0,509	-0,684	1,020	1,084	0,743	-0,462
Denmark	0,792	0,821	0,865	0,059	0,736	-0,085	1,162	0,135
Malawi	0,932	0,848	1,309	0,696	0,773	-0,646	0,448	-0,080
Chile	1,240	0,866	1,678	0,826	-0,038	0,697	0,062	-0,295
Bhutan	0,608	0,879	0,295	1,677		0,619	-0,037	0,710
Thailand	0,732	0,879	0,894	-0,825	0,348	0,670	0,406	0,831
United Kingdom	0,777	0,881	0,918	-0,120	0,361	-0,017	1,832	0,364
Trinidad and Tobago	1,385	0,943	1,122	0,241	1,232	0,750	-0,729	0,304
Austria	0,835	0,982	1,041	0,053	0,151	0,242	1,441	0,669
Tajikistan	0,749	0,988	-0,185	-1,399	1,076	1,110	0,769	0,839
Cuba	0,940	0,990	-1,333	0,374	1,230	1,707	0,256	0,910
Germany	1,164	1,009	1,357	-0,981	0,883	0,385	1,387	0,338
Dominican Republic	1,560	1,014	1,149	-0,228	1,015	1,488	0,429	-1,009
Moldova	1,020	1,030	0,781	-2,607	1,223	1,211	0,843	0,630
Kyrgyzstan	0,639	1,058	-0,330	-0,930	1,586	0,789	1,482	0,436
Bangladesh	0,867	1,076	0,518	0,562	-0,344	0,846	0,598	0,711
India	0,976	1,082	1,581	0,962	-1,535	0,754	0,501	0,635
Indonesia	1,047	1,102	0,183	-0,154	0,594	1,480	0,569	0,293
Peru	1,426	1,135	0,885	0,713	0,756	1,105	0,595	-0,383
Vietnam	0,931	1,137	-0,595	0,853	0,678	1,650	0,100	0,830
Switzerland	1,236	1,156	1,309	-0,241	0,636	0,288	1,606	0,595

	z_res_overall 26 development index	z_res_overall 26 development index, based on six dimensions	z_res_component UNDP democracy	z_res_component UNDP economic growth	z_res_component UNDP gender	z_res_component UNDP human development	z_res_component UNDP R&D	z_res_component UNDP social cohesion
New Zealand	1,037	1,158	0,681	0,509	1,070	-0,114	2,343	0,052
United States	1,069	1,294	0,516	-0,123	0,583	0,281	3,722	-0,595
Norway	1,264	1,356	0,706	0,658	1,884	0,001	1,613	0,570
Netherlands	1,409	1,369	1,748	-0,627	0,837	0,439	1,688	0,680
Costa Rica	1,949	1,377	1,930	-0,075	1,024	1,670	-0,460	0,084
Jamaica	1,687	1,401	1,703	-2,057	1,210	1,780	0,516	0,191
Finland	1,544	1,509	1,364	-0,531	1,911	0,196	2,312	0,433
Sri Lanka	2,083	1,709	1,261	0,095	1,474	1,699	0,127	0,549
Sweden	1,817	1,838	1,616	-0,120	1,656	0,273	3,077	0,519
Philippines	2,452	1,871	1,324	-1,188	2,119	1,745	1,295	0,239

Appendix Table 3. Partial correlations of smart development – development level constant. Results ordered by dependent variable

dependent variable	variable	partial correlation	Significa nce	Degrees of freedom
ecological footprint per capita	net international migration rate, 2005-2010	0,573	0,000	133
ecological footprint per capita	population density	-0,302	0,000	133
ecological footprint per capita	Immigration - Share of population 2005 (%)	0,463	0,000	133
ecological footprint per capita	military expenditures per GDP	0,321	0,001	111
ecological footprint per capita	comparative price levels (US=1.00)	0,203	0,019	131
ecological footprint per capita	years of membership in EMU, 2010	-0,188	0,029	133
Smart anti-corruption	2000 Economic Freedom Score	0,254	0,003	131
Smart anti-corruption	population density	0,240	0,005	133
Smart anti-corruption	UNDP education index	-0,235	0,006	133
Smart anti-corruption	MNC outward investments (stock) per GDP	0,245	0,011	104

Appendix Table 3. (Continued).

dependent variable	variable	partial correlation	Significa nce	Degrees of freedom
Smart anti-corruption	MNC PEN - stock of Inward FDI per GDP	0,187	0,030	133
Smart anti-corruption	military expenditures per GDP	-0,187	0,048	111
Smart avoiding high income differences	Absolute latitude	0,290	0,002	106
Smart avoiding high income differences	2000 Economic Freedom Score	-0,294	0,002	111
Smart avoiding high income differences	social security expenditure per GDP average 1990s (ILO)	0,305	0,004	85
Smart avoiding high income differences	Annual population growth rate, 1975-2005 (%)	-0,245	0,009	112
Smart avoiding high income differences	% women in government, all levels	-0,214	0,023	111
Smart avoiding high income differences	MNC PEN - stock of Inward FDI per GDP	-0,203	0,029	113
Smart avoiding high income differences	Muslim population share per total population	0,200	0,033	111
Smart avoiding Infant mortality	worker remittance inflows as % of GDP	0,389	0,000	116
Smart avoiding Infant mortality	UNDP education index	0,387	0,000	133
Smart avoiding Infant mortality	Membership in the Islamic Conference	-0,179	0,037	133
Smart avoiding to be a failed state	military expenditures per GDP	-0,396	0,000	111
Smart avoiding to be a failed state	Immigration - Share of population 2005 (%)	-0,323	0,000	133
Smart avoiding to be a failed state	military personnel rate ln (MPR+1)	-0,290	0,001	132
Smart avoiding to be a failed state	Muslim population share per total population	-0,246	0,004	132
Smart avoiding to be a failed state	% women in government, all levels	0,244	0,004	132
Smart avoiding to be a failed state	Annual population growth rate, 1975-2005 (%)	-0,242	0,005	132
Smart avoiding to be a failed state	Membership in the Islamic Conference	-0,234	0,006	133
Smart avoiding to be a failed state	MNC PEN - stock of Inward FDI per GDP	0,200	0,020	133

dependent variable	variable	partial correlation	Significa nce	Degrees of freedom
Smart avoiding to be a failed state	2000 Economic Freedom Score	0,193	0,026	131
Smart avoiding to be a failed state	MNC outward investments (stock) per GDP	0,194	0,046	104
Smart avoiding unemployment	Muslim population share per total population	-0,299	0,001	118
Smart avoiding unemployment	foreign savings rate	-0,204	0,025	118
Smart avoiding unemployment	military personnel rate ln (MPR+1)	-0,201	0,028	118
Smart avoiding unemployment	public education expenditure per GNP	-0,204	0,029	113
Smart civil and political liberties	Membership in the Islamic Conference	-0,386	0,000	132
Smart civil and political liberties	Muslim population share per total population	-0,405	0,000	131
Smart civil and political liberties	military expenditures per GDP	-0,387	0,000	111
Smart civil and political liberties	military personnel rate ln (MPR+1)	-0,479	0,000	131
Smart civil and political liberties	Immigration - Share of population 2005 (%)	-0,380	0,000	132
Smart civil and political liberties	2000 Economic Freedom Score	0,380	0,000	130
Smart civil and political liberties	% women in government, all levels	0,447	0,000	131
Smart civil and political liberties	net international migration rate, 2005-2010	-0,263	0,002	132
Smart civil and political liberties	Annual population growth rate, 1975-2005 (%)	-0,242	0,005	131
Smart closing economic gender gap	Membership in the Islamic Conference	-0,415	0,000	117
Smart closing economic gender gap	Muslim population share per total population	-0,529	0,000	115
Smart closing economic gender gap	Annual population growth rate, 1975-2005 (%)	-0,442	0,000	116
Smart closing economic gender gap	military personnel rate ln (MPR+1)	-0,316	0,000	117
Smart closing economic gender gap	% women in government, all levels	0,408	0,000	116
Smart closing economic gender gap	UNDP education index	0,446	0,000	117
Smart closing economic gender gap	social security expenditure per GDP average 1990s (ILO)	0,273	0,008	90

Appendix Table 3. (Continued).

dependent variable	variable	partial correlation	Significance	Degrees of freedom
Smart closing economic gender gap	MNC outward investments (stock) per GDP	0,225	0,025	97
Smart closing economic gender gap	military expenditures per GDP	-0,213	0,030	102
Smart closing economic gender gap	net international migration rate, 2005-2010	-0,197	0,031	117
Smart closing economic gender gap	public education expenditure per GNP	0,184	0,048	114
Smart closing educational gender gap	Membership in the Islamic Conference	-0,336	0,000	117
Smart closing educational gender gap	UNDP education index	0,679	0,000	117
Smart closing educational gender gap	worker remittance inflows as % of GDP	0,306	0,001	105
Smart closing educational gender gap	Muslim population share per total population	-0,270	0,003	115
Smart closing health and survivial gender gap	% world population	-0,370	0,000	117
Smart closing health and survivial gender gap	population density	-0,250	0,006	117
Smart closing health and survivial gender gap	% women in government, all levels	0,214	0,020	116
Smart closing of global gender gap overall score	Membership in the Islamic Conference	-0,449	0,000	117
Smart closing of global gender gap overall score	Muslim population share per total population	-0,515	0,000	115
Smart closing of global gender gap overall score	Annual population growth rate, 1975-2005 (%)	-0,354	0,000	116
Smart closing of global gender gap overall score	military personnel rate ln (MPR+1)	-0,363	0,000	117
Smart closing of global gender gap overall score	% women in government, all levels	0,416	0,000	116
Smart closing of global gender gap overall score	UNDP education index	0,481	0,000	117
Smart closing of global gender gap overall score	military expenditures per GDP	-0,333	0,001	102
Smart closing of global gender gap overall score	social security expenditure per GDP average 1990s (ILO)	0,338	0,001	90
Smart closing of global gender gap overall score	Immigration - Share of population 2005 (%)	-0,254	0,005	117

dependent variable	variable	partial correlation	Significa nce	Degrees of freedom
Smart closing of global gender gap overall score	public education expenditure per GNP	0,209	0,024	114
Smart closing of global gender gap overall score	net international migration rate, 2005-2010	-0,200	0,029	117
Smart closing political gender gap	military personnel rate ln (MPR+1)	-0,329	0,000	117
Smart closing political gender gap	military personnel rate ln (MPR+1)	-0,329	0,000	117
Smart closing political gender gap	social security expenditure per GDP average 1990s (ILO)	0,344	0,001	90
Smart closing political gender gap	Immigration - Share of population 2005 (%)	-0,307	0,001	117
Smart closing political gender gap	% women in government, all levels	0,298	0,001	116
Smart closing political gender gap	social security expenditure per GDP average 1990s (ILO)	0,344	0,001	90
Smart closing political gender gap	Immigration - Share of population 2005 (%)	-0,307	0,001	117
Smart closing political gender gap	% women in government, all levels	0,298	0,001	116
Smart closing political gender gap	military expenditures per GDP	-0,291	0,003	102
Smart closing political gender gap	military expenditures per GDP	-0,291	0,003	102
Smart closing political gender gap	Muslim population share per total population	-0,264	0,004	115
Smart closing political gender gap	Muslim population share per total population	-0,264	0,004	115
Smart closing political gender gap	Membership in the Islamic Conference	-0,213	0,020	117
Smart closing political gender gap	Membership in the Islamic Conference	-0,213	0,020	117
Smart democracy measure	Membership in the Islamic Conference	-0,450	0,000	127
Smart democracy measure	Muslim population share per total population	-0,452	0,000	127
Smart democracy measure	military expenditures per GDP	-0,362	0,000	106
Smart democracy measure	military personnel rate ln (MPR+1)	-0,395	0,000	126
Smart democracy measure	Immigration - Share of population 2005 (%)	-0,388	0,000	127

Appendix Table 3. (Continued).

dependent variable	variable	partial correlation	Significance	Degrees of freedom
Smart democracy measure	2000 Economic Freedom Score	0,361	0,000	125
Smart democracy measure	% women in government, all levels	0,400	0,000	126
Smart democracy measure	net international migration rate, 2005-2010	-0,289	0,001	127
Smart democracy measure	Annual population growth rate, 1975-2005 (%)	-0,257	0,003	126
Smart democracy measure	Openness-Index, 1990 (export-share per GDP + import-share per GDP)	-0,197	0,026	125
Smart economic growth IMF 2010	worker remittance inflows as % of GDP	-0,272	0,003	115
Smart economic growth IMF 2010	Annual population growth rate, 1975-2005 (%)	0,233	0,007	129
Smart economic growth IMF 2010	Muslim population share per total population	0,180	0,040	129
Smart economic growth IMF 2010	net international migration rate, 2005-2010	0,178	0,041	131
Smart economic growth in real terms pc. per annum, 1990-2005	% world population	0,311	0,000	131
Smart economic growth in real terms pc. per annum, 1990-2005	public education expenditure per GNP	-0,305	0,001	122
Smart economic growth in real terms pc. per annum, 1990-2005	social security expenditure per GDP average 1990s (ILO)	-0,291	0,004	94
Smart economic growth in real terms pc. per annum, 1990-2005	worker remittance inflows as % of GDP	-0,231	0,013	114
Smart economic growth in real terms pc. per annum, 1990-2005	MNC PEN - stock of Inward FDI per GDP	0,179	0,039	131
Smart female survival probability of surviving to age 65	worker remittance inflows as % of GDP	0,401	0,000	116
Smart female survival probability of surviving to age 65	public education expenditure per GNP	-0,271	0,002	124

dependent variable	variable	partial correlation	Significa nce	Degrees of freedom
Smart female survival probability of surviving to age 65	MNC PEN - stock of Inward FDI per GDP	-0,173	0,044	133
Smart female survival probability of surviving to age 65	Muslim population share per total population	0,174	0,046	131
Smart gender empowerment	Membership in the Islamic Conference	-0,493	0,000	71
Smart gender empowerment	Muslim population share per total population	-0,490	0,000	69
Smart gender empowerment	military expenditures per GDP	-0,501	0,000	61
Smart gender empowerment	military personnel rate ln (MPR+1)	-0,520	0,000	71
Smart gender empowerment	% women in government, all levels	0,427	0,000	69
Smart gender empowerment	Annual population growth rate, 1975-2005 (%)	-0,344	0,003	70
Smart gender empowerment	Immigration - Share of population 2005 (%)	-0,327	0,005	71
Smart gender empowerment	social security expenditure per GDP average 1990s (ILO)	0,349	0,006	58
Smart gender empowerment	UNDP education index	0,279	0,017	71
Smart global tolerance	social security expenditure per GDP average 1990s (ILO)	0,502	0,000	52
Smart global tolerance	military personnel rate ln (MPR+1)	-0,495	0,000	66
Smart global tolerance	Muslim population share per total population	-0,329	0,006	66
Smart global tolerance	Membership in the Islamic Conference	-0,319	0,008	66
Smart global tolerance	MNC outward investments (stock) per GDP	0,302	0,021	56
Smart global tolerance	public education expenditure per GNP	0,256	0,036	65
Smart happy life years	worker remittance inflows as % of GDP	0,333	0,000	116
Smart happy life years	military expenditures per GDP	-0,204	0,030	111
Smart Human development index	worker remittance inflows as % of GDP	0,409	0,000	116
Smart Human development index	UNDP education index	0,504	0,000	133

Appendix Table 3. (Continued).

dependent variable	variable	partial correlation	Significance	Degrees of freedom
Smart Human development index	Annual population growth rate, 1975-2005 (%)	-0,214	0,013	132
Smart Human development index	net international migration rate, 2005-2010	-0,188	0,029	133
Smart Human development index	Membership in the Islamic Conference	-0,178	0,039	133
Smart life expectancy (years)	worker remittance inflows as % of GDP	0,411	0,000	116
Smart life expectancy (years)	public education expenditure per GNP	-0,236	0,008	124
Smart life expectancy (years)	UNDP education index	0,198	0,021	133
Smart life satisfaction	worker remittance inflows as % of GDP	0,281	0,002	116
Smart life satisfaction	military expenditures per GDP	-0,196	0,038	111
smart overall development index	Membership in the Islamic Conference	-0,346	0,000	133
smart overall development index	Muslim population share per total population	-0,326	0,000	132
smart overall development index	military expenditures per GDP	-0,389	0,000	111
smart overall development index	Immigration - Share of population 2005 (%)	-0,336	0,000	133
smart overall development index	military personnel rate ln (MPR+1)	-0,284	0,001	132
smart overall development index	UNDP education index	0,276	0,001	133
smart overall development index	% women in government, all levels	0,268	0,002	132
smart overall development index	Annual population growth rate, 1975-2005 (%)	-0,256	0,003	132
smart overall development index	worker remittance inflows as % of GDP	0,244	0,008	116
smart overall development index	net international migration rate, 2005-2010	-0,215	0,012	133
smart overall development index	2000 Economic Freedom Score	0,200	0,021	131
Smart per capita world class universities	social security expenditure per GDP average 1990s (ILO)	0,351	0,000	96

dependent variable	variable	partial correlation	Significa nce	Degrees of freedom
Smart per capita world class universities	MNC outward investments (stock) per GDP	0,359	0,000	104
Smart per capita world class universities	Openness-Index, 1990 (export-share per GDP + import-share per GDP)	-0,234	0,007	131
Smart per capita world class universities	FPZ (free production zones) employment as % of total population	-0,200	0,020	133
Smart per capita world class universities	public education expenditure per GNP	0,202	0,024	124
Smart per capita world class universities	% women in government, all levels	0,187	0,030	132
Smart rule of law	2000 Economic Freedom Score	0,325	0,000	131
Smart tertiary enrollment	Annual population growth rate, 1975-2005 (%)	-0,439	0,000	119
Smart tertiary enrollment	social security expenditure per GDP average 1990s (ILO)	0,379	0,000	90
Smart tertiary enrollment	Absolute latitude	0,385	0,000	114
Smart tertiary enrollment	UNDP education index	0,439	0,000	120
Smart tertiary enrollment	net international migration rate, 2005-2010	-0,221	0,014	120
Smart tertiary enrollment	worker remittance inflows as % of GDP	0,235	0,015	106
Smart tertiary enrollment	military expenditures per GDP	-0,203	0,037	104
Smart tertiary enrollment	Openness-Index, 1990 (export-share per GDP + import-share per GDP)	-0,190	0,037	118
Smart tertiary enrollment	Membership in the Islamic Conference	-0,188	0,038	120
Smart tertiary enrollment	FPZ (free production zones) employment as % of total population	-0,182	0,045	120
Smart civil and political liberties	% women in government, all levels	0,447	0,000	131
Smart closing economic gender gap	% women in government, all levels	0,408	0,000	116
Smart closing of global gender gap overall score	% women in government, all levels	0,416	0,000	116
Smart democracy measure	% women in government, all levels	0,400	0,000	126

Appendix Table 3. (Continued).

dependent variable	variable	partial correlation	Significa nce	Degrees of freedom
Smart gender empowerment	% women in government, all levels	0,427	0,000	69
Smart closing political gender gap	% women in government, all levels	0,298	0,001	116
smart overall development index	% women in government, all levels	0,268	0,002	132
Smart avoiding to be a failed state	% women in government, all levels	0,244	0,004	132
Smart closing health and survivial gender gap	% women in government, all levels	0,214	0,020	116
Smart avoiding high income differences	% women in government, all levels	-0,214	0,023	111
Smart per capita world class universities	% women in government, all levels	0,187	0,030	132
Smart closing health and survivial gender gap	% world population	-0,370	0,000	117
Smart economic growth in real terms pc. per annum, 1990-2005	% world population	0,311	0,000	131
Smart civil and political liberties	2000 Economic Freedom Score	0,380	0,000	130
Smart democracy measure	2000 Economic Freedom Score	0,361	0,000	125
Smart rule of law	2000 Economic Freedom Score	0,325	0,000	131
Smart avoiding high income differences	2000 Economic Freedom Score	-0,294	0,002	111
Smart anti-corruption	2000 Economic Freedom Score	0,254	0,003	131
smart overall development index	2000 Economic Freedom Score	0,200	0,021	131
Smart avoiding to be a failed state	2000 Economic Freedom Score	0,193	0,026	131
Smart tertiary enrollment	Absolute latitude	0,385	0,000	114
Smart avoiding high income differences	Absolute latitude	0,290	0,002	106
Smart closing economic gender gap	Annual population growth rate, 1975-2005 (%)	-0,442	0,000	116
Smart closing of global gender gap overall score	Annual population growth rate, 1975-2005 (%)	-0,354	0,000	116

dependent variable	variable	partial correlation	Significa nce	Degrees of freedom
Smart tertiary enrollment	Annual population growth rate, 1975-2005 (%)	-0,439	0,000	119
Smart democracy measure	Annual population growth rate, 1975-2005 (%)	-0,257	0,003	126
Smart gender empowerment	Annual population growth rate, 1975-2005 (%)	-0,344	0,003	70
smart overall development index	Annual population growth rate, 1975-2005 (%)	-0,256	0,003	132
Smart avoiding to be a failed state	Annual population growth rate, 1975-2005 (%)	-0,242	0,005	132
Smart civil and political liberties	Annual population growth rate, 1975-2005 (%)	-0,242	0,005	131
Smart economic growth IMF 2010	Annual population growth rate, 1975-2005 (%)	0,233	0,007	129
Smart avoiding high income differences	Annual population growth rate, 1975-2005 (%)	-0,245	0,009	112
Smart Human development index	Annual population growth rate, 1975-2005 (%)	-0,214	0,013	132
ecological footprint per capita	comparative price levels (US=1.00)	0,203	0,019	131
Smart avoiding unemployment	foreign savings rate	-0,204	0,025	118
Smart per capita world class universities	FPZ (free production zones) employment as % of total population	-0,200	0,020	133
Smart tertiary enrollment	FPZ (free production zones) employment as % of total population	-0,182	0,045	120
Smart avoiding to be a failed state	Immigration - Share of population 2005 (%)	-0,323	0,000	133
Smart civil and political liberties	Immigration - Share of population 2005 (%)	-0,380	0,000	132
Smart democracy measure	Immigration - Share of population 2005 (%)	-0,388	0,000	127
smart overall development index	Immigration - Share of population 2005 (%)	-0,336	0,000	133
ecological footprint per capita	Immigration - Share of population 2005 (%)	0,463	0,000	133
Smart closing political gender gap	Immigration - Share of population 2005 (%)	-0,307	0,001	117
Smart closing political gender gap	Immigration - Share of population 2005 (%)	-0,307	0,001	117
Smart closing of global gender gap overall score	Immigration - Share of population 2005 (%)	-0,254	0,005	117

Appendix Table 3. (Continued).

dependent variable	variable	partial correlation	Significance	Degrees of freedom
Smart gender empowerment	Immigration - Share of population 2005 (%)	-0,327	0,005	71
Smart civil and political liberties	Membership in the Islamic Conference	-0,386	0,000	132
Smart closing economic gender gap	Membership in the Islamic Conference	-0,415	0,000	117
Smart closing educational gender gap	Membership in the Islamic Conference	-0,336	0,000	117
Smart closing of global gender gap overall score	Membership in the Islamic Conference	-0,449	0,000	117
Smart democracy measure	Membership in the Islamic Conference	-0,450	0,000	127
Smart gender empowerment	Membership in the Islamic Conference	-0,493	0,000	71
smart overall development index	Membership in the Islamic Conference	-0,346	0,000	133
Smart avoiding to be a failed state	Membership in the Islamic Conference	-0,234	0,006	133
Smart global tolerance	Membership in the Islamic Conference	-0,319	0,008	66
Smart closing political gender gap	Membership in the Islamic Conference	-0,213	0,020	117
Smart closing political gender gap	Membership in the Islamic Conference	-0,213	0,020	117
Smart avoiding Infant mortality	Membership in the Islamic Conference	-0,179	0,037	133
Smart tertiary enrollment	Membership in the Islamic Conference	-0,188	0,038	120
Smart Human development index	Membership in the Islamic Conference	-0,178	0,039	133
Smart avoiding to be a failed state	military expenditures per GDP	-0,396	0,000	111
Smart civil and political liberties	military expenditures per GDP	-0,387	0,000	111
Smart democracy measure	military expenditures per GDP	-0,362	0,000	106
Smart gender empowerment	military expenditures per GDP	-0,501	0,000	61
smart overall development index	military expenditures per GDP	-0,389	0,000	111

dependent variable	variable	partial correlation	Significa nce	Degrees of freedom
Smart closing of global gender gap overall score	military expenditures per GDP	-0,333	0,001	102
ecological footprint per capita	military expenditures per GDP	0,321	0,001	111
Smart closing political gender gap	military expenditures per GDP	-0,291	0,003	102
Smart closing economic gender gap	military expenditures per GDP	-0,213	0,030	102
Smart happy life years	military expenditures per GDP	-0,204	0,030	111
Smart tertiary enrollment	military expenditures per GDP	-0,203	0,037	104
Smart life satisfaction	military expenditures per GDP	-0,196	0,038	111
Smart anti-corruption	military expenditures per GDP	-0,187	0,048	111
Smart civil and political liberties	military personnel rate ln (MPR+1)	-0,479	0,000	131
Smart closing economic gender gap	military personnel rate ln (MPR+1)	-0,316	0,000	117
Smart closing of global gender gap overall score	military personnel rate ln (MPR+1)	-0,363	0,000	117
Smart closing political gender gap	military personnel rate ln (MPR+1)	-0,329	0,000	117
Smart closing political gender gap	military personnel rate ln (MPR+1)	-0,329	0,000	117
Smart democracy measure	military personnel rate ln (MPR+1)	-0,395	0,000	126
Smart gender empowerment	military personnel rate ln (MPR+1)	-0,520	0,000	71
Smart global tolerance	military personnel rate ln (MPR+1)	-0,495	0,000	66
Smart avoiding to be a failed state	military personnel rate ln (MPR+1)	-0,290	0,001	132
smart overall development index	military personnel rate ln (MPR+1)	-0,284	0,001	132
Smart avoiding unemployment	military personnel rate ln (MPR+1)	-0,201	0,028	118
Smart per capita world class universities	MNC outward investments (stock) per GDP	0,359	0,000	104

Appendix Table 3. (Continued).

dependent variable	variable	partial correlation	Significance	Degrees of freedom
Smart anti-corruption	MNC outward investments (stock) per GDP	0,245	0,011	104
Smart global tolerance	MNC outward investments (stock) per GDP	0,302	0,021	56
Smart closing economic gender gap	MNC outward investments (stock) per GDP	0,225	0,025	97
Smart avoiding to be a failed state	MNC outward investments (stock) per GDP	0,194	0,046	104
Smart avoiding to be a failed state	MNC PEN - stock of Inward FDI per GDP	0,200	0,020	133
Smart avoiding high income differences	MNC PEN - stock of Inward FDI per GDP	-0,203	0,029	113
Smart anti-corruption	MNC PEN - stock of Inward FDI per GDP	0,187	0,030	133
Smart economic growth in real terms pc. per annum, 1990-2005	MNC PEN - stock of Inward FDI per GDP	0,179	0,039	131
Smart female survival probability of surviving to age 65	MNC PEN - stock of Inward FDI per GDP	-0,173	0,044	133
Smart civil and political liberties	Muslim population share per total population	-0,405	0,000	131
Smart closing economic gender gap	Muslim population share per total population	-0,529	0,000	115
Smart closing of global gender gap overall score	Muslim population share per total population	-0,515	0,000	115
Smart democracy measure	Muslim population share per total population	-0,452	0,000	127
Smart gender empowerment	Muslim population share per total population	-0,490	0,000	69
smart overall development index	Muslim population share per total population	-0,326	0,000	132
Smart avoiding unemployment	Muslim population share per total population	-0,299	0,001	118
Smart closing educational gender gap	Muslim population share per total population	-0,270	0,003	115
Smart avoiding to be a failed state	Muslim population share per total population	-0,246	0,004	132
Smart closing political gender gap	Muslim population share per total population	-0,264	0,004	115
Smart closing political gender gap	Muslim population share per total population	-0,264	0,004	115

dependent variable	variable	partial correlation	Significance	Degrees of freedom
Smart global tolerance	Muslim population share per total population	-0,329	0,006	66
Smart avoiding high income differences	Muslim population share per total population	0,200	0,033	111
Smart economic growth IMF 2010	Muslim population share per total population	0,180	0,040	129
Smart female survival probability of surviving to age 65	Muslim population share per total population	0,174	0,046	131
ecological footprint per capita	net international migration rate, 2005-2010	0,573	0,000	133
Smart democracy measure	net international migration rate, 2005-2010	-0,289	0,001	127
Smart civil and political liberties	net international migration rate, 2005-2010	-0,263	0,002	132
smart overall development index	net international migration rate, 2005-2010	-0,215	0,012	133
Smart tertiary enrollment	net international migration rate, 2005-2010	-0,221	0,014	120
Smart closing of global gender gap overall score	net international migration rate, 2005-2010	-0,200	0,029	117
Smart Human development index	net international migration rate, 2005-2010	-0,188	0,029	133
Smart closing economic gender gap	net international migration rate, 2005-2010	-0,197	0,031	117
Smart economic growth IMF 2010	net international migration rate, 2005-2010	0,178	0,041	131
Smart per capita world class universities	Openness-Index, 1990 (export-share per GDP + import-share per GDP)	-0,234	0,007	131
Smart democracy measure	Openness-Index, 1990 (export-share per GDP + import-share per GDP)	-0,197	0,026	125
Smart tertiary enrollment	Openness-Index, 1990 (export-share per GDP + import-share per GDP)	-0,190	0,037	118
ecological footprint per capita	population density	-0,302	0,000	133
Smart anti-corruption	population density	0,240	0,005	133
Smart closing health and survivial gender gap	population density	-0,250	0,006	117

Appendix Table 3. (Continued).

dependent variable	variable	partial correlation	Significance	Degrees of freedom
Smart economic growth in real terms pc. per annum, 1990-2005	public education expenditure per GNP	-0,305	0,001	122
Smart female survival probability of surviving to age 65	public education expenditure per GNP	-0,271	0,002	124
Smart life expectancy (years)	public education expenditure per GNP	-0,236	0,008	124
Smart closing of global gender gap overall score	public education expenditure per GNP	0,209	0,024	114
Smart per capita world class universities	public education expenditure per GNP	0,202	0,024	124
Smart avoiding unemployment	public education expenditure per GNP	-0,204	0,029	113
Smart global tolerance	public education expenditure per GNP	0,256	0,036	65
Smart closing economic gender gap	public education expenditure per GNP	0,184	0,048	114
Smart global tolerance	social security expenditure per GDP average 1990s (ILO)	0,502	0,000	52
Smart per capita world class universities	social security expenditure per GDP average 1990s (ILO)	0,351	0,000	96
Smart tertiary enrollment	social security expenditure per GDP average 1990s (ILO)	0,379	0,000	90
Smart closing of global gender gap overall score	social security expenditure per GDP average 1990s (ILO)	0,338	0,001	90
Smart closing political gender gap	social security expenditure per GDP average 1990s (ILO)	0,344	0,001	90
Smart closing political gender gap	social security expenditure per GDP average 1990s (ILO)	0,344	0,001	90
Smart economic growth in real terms pc. per annum, 1990-2005	social security expenditure per GDP average 1990s (ILO)	-0,291	0,004	94
Smart avoiding high income differences	social security expenditure per GDP average 1990s (ILO)	0,305	0,004	85
Smart gender empowerment	social security expenditure per GDP average 1990s (ILO)	0,349	0,006	58
Smart closing economic gender gap	social security expenditure per GDP average 1990s (ILO)	0,273	0,008	90

dependent variable	variable	partial correlation	Significa nce	Degrees of freedom
Smart closing economic gender gap	UNDP education index	0,446	0,000	117
Smart closing educational gender gap	UNDP education index	0,679	0,000	117
Smart closing of global gender gap overall score	UNDP education index	0,481	0,000	117
Smart Human development index	UNDP education index	0,504	0,000	133
Smart avoiding Infant mortality	UNDP education index	0,387	0,000	133
Smart tertiary enrollment	UNDP education index	0,439	0,000	120
smart overall development index	UNDP education index	0,276	0,001	133
Smart anti-corruption	UNDP education index	-0,235	0,006	133
Smart gender empowerment	UNDP education index	0,279	0,017	71
Smart life expectancy (years)	UNDP education index	0,198	0,021	133
Smart female survival probability of surviving to age 65	worker remittance inflows as % of GDP	0,401	0,000	116
Smart happy life years	worker remittance inflows as % of GDP	0,333	0,000	116
Smart Human development index	worker remittance inflows as % of GDP	0,409	0,000	116
Smart avoiding Infant mortality	worker remittance inflows as % of GDP	0,389	0,000	116
Smart life expectancy (years)	worker remittance inflows as % of GDP	0,411	0,000	116
Smart closing educational gender gap	worker remittance inflows as % of GDP	0,306	0,001	105
Smart life satisfaction	worker remittance inflows as % of GDP	0,281	0,002	116
Smart economic growth IMF 2010	worker remittance inflows as % of GDP	-0,272	0,003	115
smart overall development index	worker remittance inflows as % of GDP	0,244	0,008	116
Smart economic growth in real terms pc. per annum, 1990-2005	worker remittance inflows as % of GDP	-0,231	0,013	114
Smart tertiary enrollment	worker remittance inflows as % of GDP	0,235	0,015	106
ecological footprint per capita	years of membership in EMU, 2010	-0,188	0,029	133

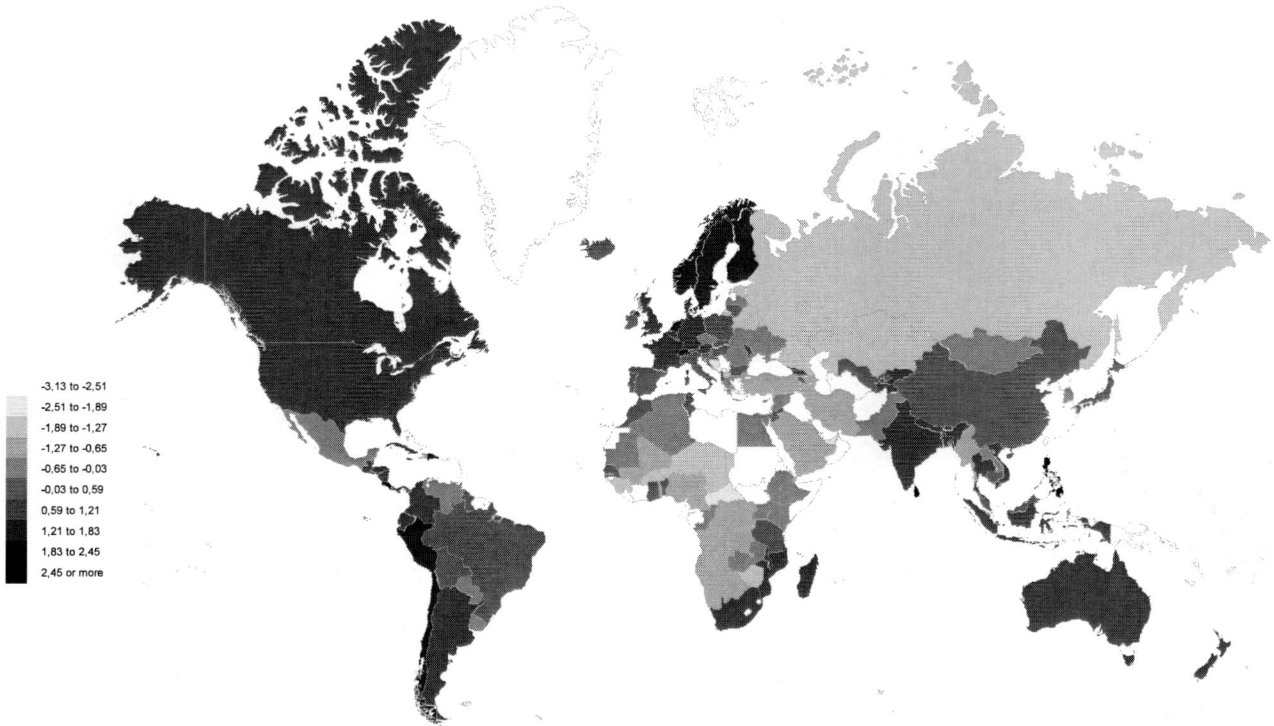

Source: Our own calculations and http://www.clearlyandsimply.com/

Appendix Map 1. z_res_overall 26 development index.

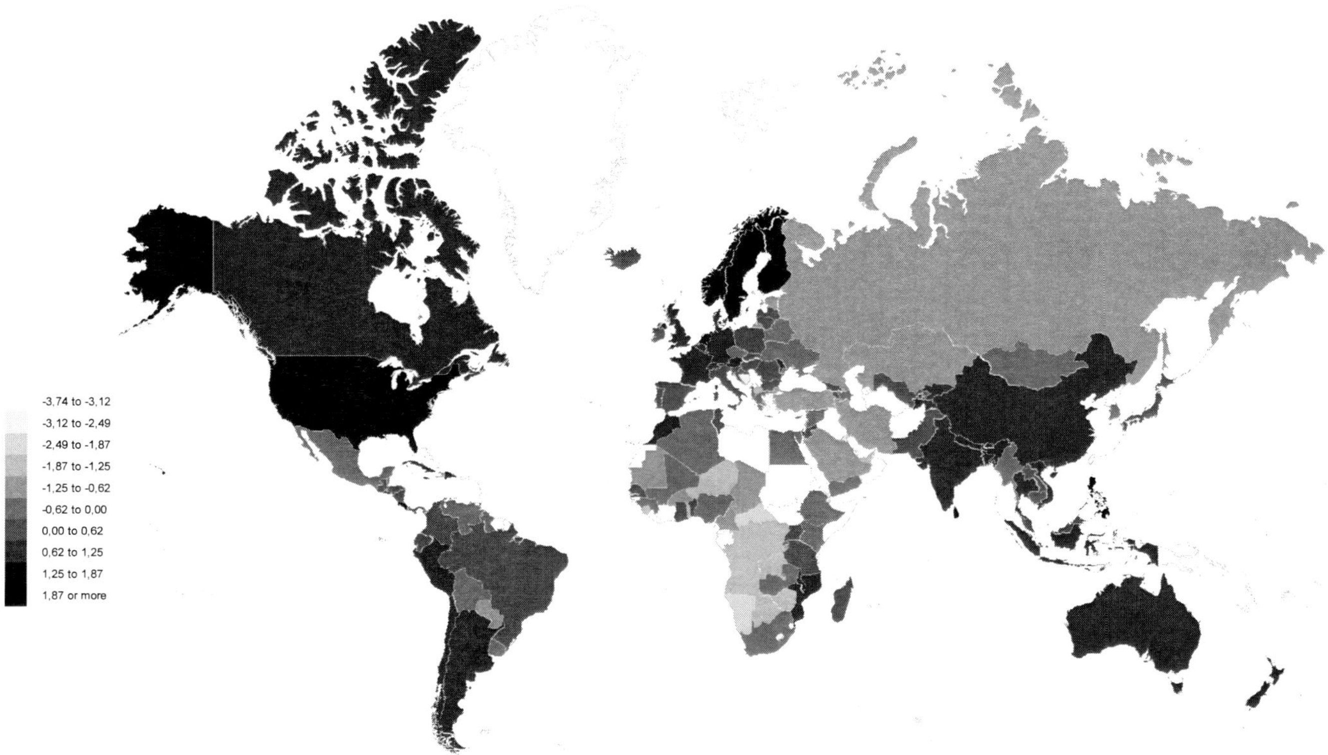

Source: Our own calculations and http://www.clearlyandsimply.com/

Appendix Map 2. z_res_overall 26 development index, based on six dimensions.

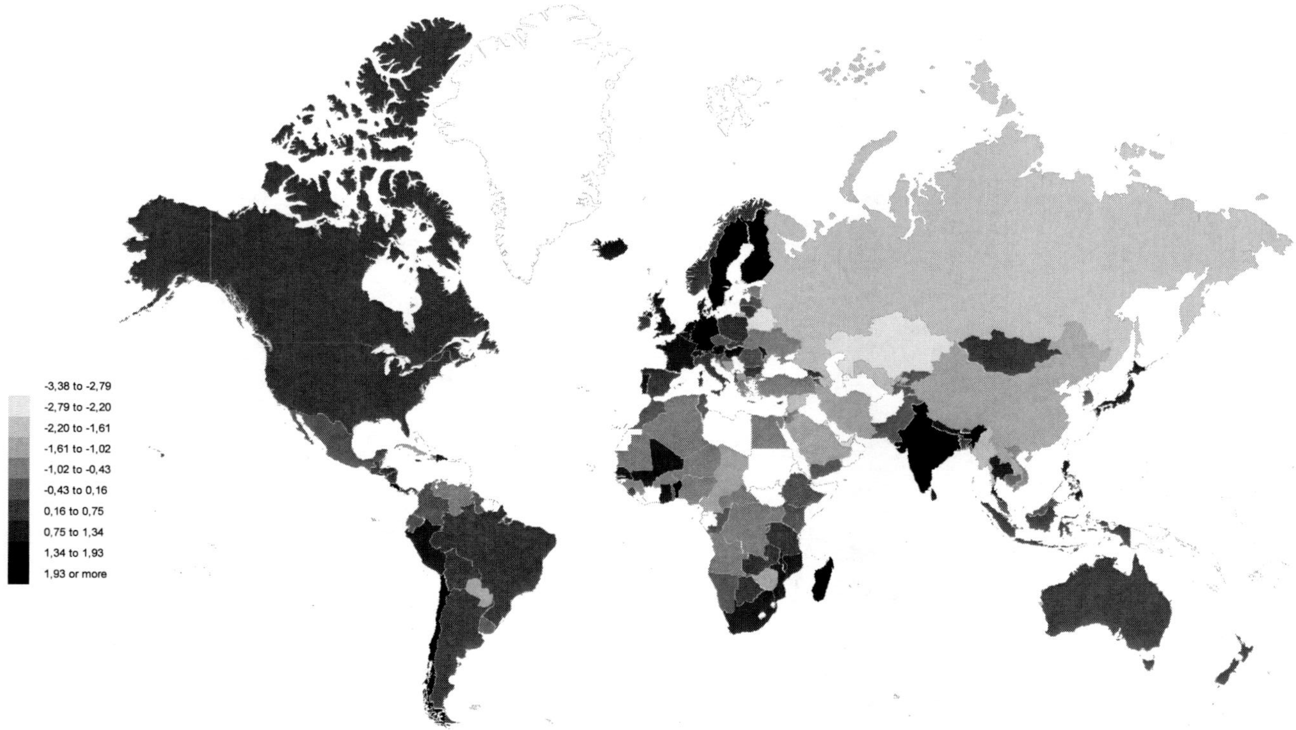

Source: Our own calculations and http://www.clearlyandsimply.com/

Appendix Map 3. z_res_component UNDP democracy.

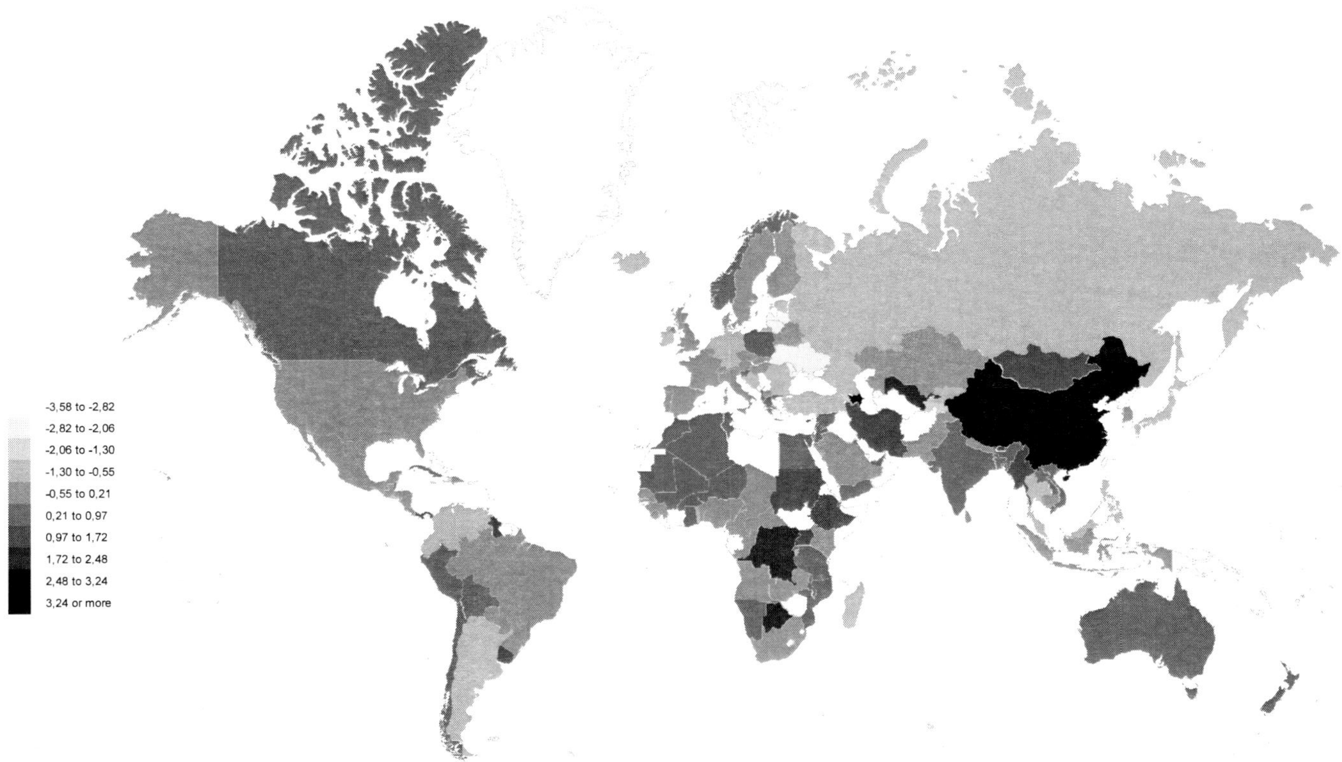

Source: Our own calculations and http://www.clearlyandsimply.com/

Appendix Map 4. z_res_component UNDP economic growth.

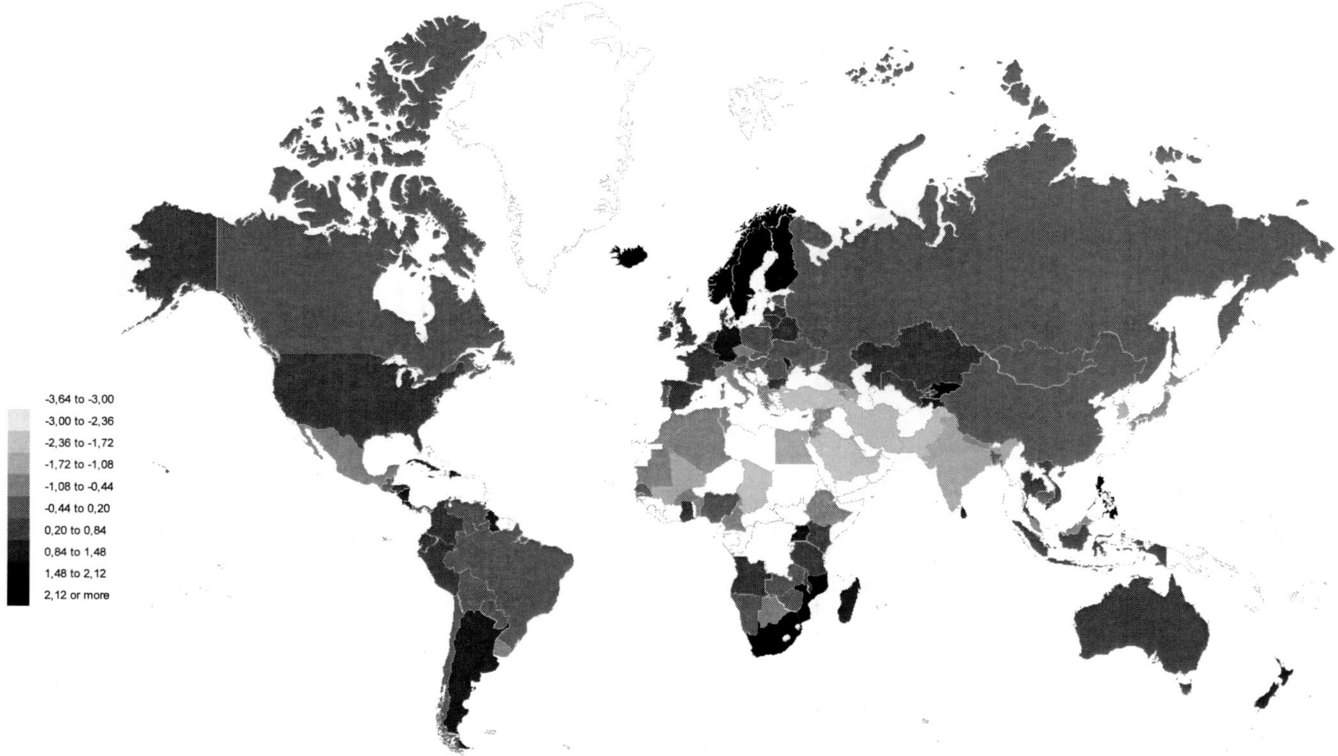

Source: Our own calculations and http://www.clearlyandsimply.com/

Appendix Map 5. z_res_component UNDP gender.

Source: Our own calculations and http://www.clearlyandsimply.com/

Appendix Map 6. z_res_component UNDP human development.

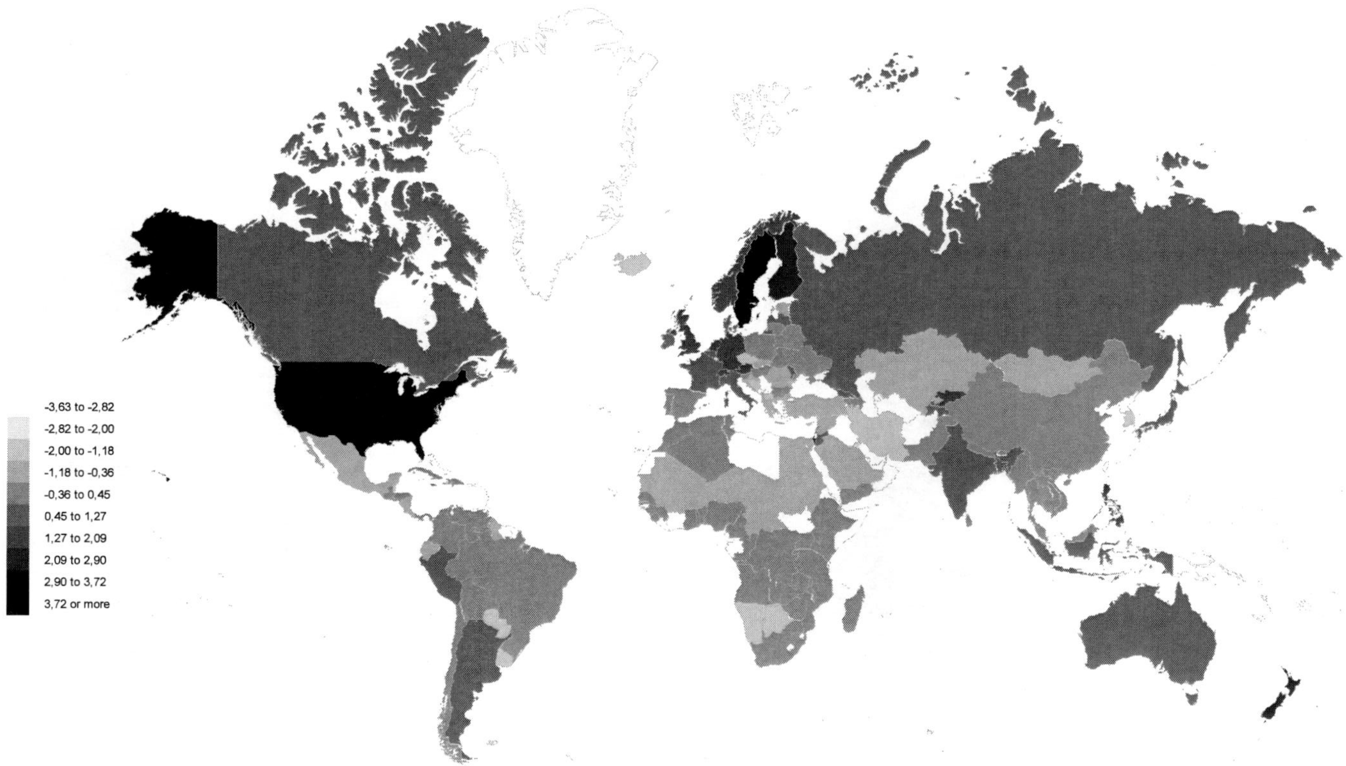

Source: Our own calculations and http://www.clearlyandsimply.com/

Appendix Map 7. z_res_component UNDP R&D.

Source: Our own calculations and http://www.clearlyandsimply.com/

Appendix Map 8. z_res_component UNDP social cohesion.

Appendix Table 4. Rankings. Global smart development

	smart	smart	smart	smart	smart	smart	smart	smart
	26 development index	26 development index, based on six dimensions	democracy	economic growth	gender	human development	R&D	social cohesion
Philippines	1	1	11	126	1	2	13	69
Sri Lanka	2	3	14	63	9	4	60	37
Costa Rica	3	6	1	76	18	5	101	85
Sweden	**4**	**2**	**5**	**81**	**6**	**61**	**2**	**38**
Jamaica	5	5	3	135	14	1	30	75
Dominican Republic	6	19	16	89	20	7	36	123
Finland	**7**	**4**	**9**	**103**	**3**	**65**	**4**	**42**
Peru	8	13	28	29	28	18	25	108
Netherlands	**9**	**7**	**2**	**108**	**24**	**48**	**7**	**20**
Trinidad and Tobago	10	24	17	55	11	34	116	59
Norway	11	8	37	33	4	81	8	36
Chile	12	28	4	23	66	38	67	104
Switzerland	13	11	12	90	33	57	9	31
Germany	**14**	**20**	**10**	**122**	**21**	**52**	**12**	**56**
El Salvador	15	36	31	118	29	12	63	112
United States	16	9	46	82	38	58	1	114
Indonesia	17	14	68	84	37	8	27	61
New Zealand	18	10	39	41	16	92	3	86
Moldova	19	18	34	139	13	10	19	26
Argentina	20	31	47	111	19	19	21	111
India	21	15	6	18	112	33	31	25
Cuba	22	21	124	48	12	3	46	6

	smart	smart	smart	smart	smart	smart	smart	smart
	26 development index	26 development index, based on six dimensions	democracy	economic growth	gender	human development	R&D	social cohesion
Malawi	23	29	13	30	27	109	34	96
Vietnam	24	12	106	22	32	6	64	11
Colombia	25	60	76	113	34	9	54	124
Bangladesh	26	16	45	37	80	27	24	17
Honduras	27	44	53	95	36	25	83	94
Austria	**28**	**23**	**19**	**69**	**56**	**62**	**11**	**23**
Denmark	**29**	**30**	**29**	**66**	**31**	**88**	**16**	**81**
United Kingdom	**30**	**25**	**25**	**80**	**47**	**85**	**6**	**54**
Panama	31	55	49	11	54	43	95	117
Tajikistan	32	22	86	132	15	17	20	8
Thailand	33	26	26	115	48	39	37	10
Nicaragua	34	41	56	97	23	32	103	43
Guatemala	35	48	52	104	69	11	86	99
Belgium	**36**	**33**	**33**	**75**	**45**	**72**	**15**	**60**
Nepal	37	38	24	86	84	41	41	88
South Africa	38	80	15	101	2	119	78	125
France	**39**	**37**	**32**	**65**	**41**	**71**	**23**	**63**
Kyrgyzstan	40	17	93	119	8	30	10	41
Madagascar	41	43	8	131	17	104	77	45
Canada	42	35	38	34	55	87	17	83

Appendix Table 4. (Continued).

	smart	smart	smart	smart	smart	smart	smart	smart
	26 development index	26 development index, based on six dimensions	democracy	economic growth	gender	human development	R&D	social cohesion
Bhutan	43	27	61	6		40	76	18
Australia	44	34	43	32	50	78	18	90
Ecuador	45	76	82	116	25	23	124	107
Mozambique	46	32	22	36	5	128	70	16
Tunisia	47	47	80	24	85	15	55	103
Morocco	48	39	72	45	96	13	50	84
Ghana	49	49	20	21	49	106	94	87
Brazil	50	74	50	93	68	31	93	120
Senegal	51	45	18	62	58	102	89	33
Belize	52	82	60	52	74	35	127	113
China	53	40	122	1	81	22	81	51
Georgia	54	42	66	112	97	14	14	101
Ireland	**55**	**57**	**40**	**114**	**42**	**86**	**28**	**57**
Iceland	56	63	30	125	7	79	130	49
Bulgaria	**57**	**51**	**54**	**121**	**40**	**50**	**53**	**48**
Guyana	58	81	73	15	22	98	122	115
Slovakia	**59**	**65**	**51**	**59**	**65**	**56**	**107**	**68**
Hungary	**60**	**52**	**21**	**99**	**72**	**80**	**57**	**35**
Poland	**61**	**59**	**65**	**27**	**67**	**74**	**51**	**76**
Jordan	62	50	99	39	87	21	32	92
Cambodia	63	54	77	91	59	93	62	13
Tanzania	64	61	48	20	35	124	85	32

	smart	smart	smart	smart	smart	smart	smart	smart
	26 development index	26 development index, based on six dimensions	democracy	economic growth	gender	human development	R&D	social cohesion
Israel	65	46	84	57	83	70	5	74
Spain	**66**	**64**	**57**	**67**	**52**	**77**	**59**	**80**
Bolivia	67	92	62	50	76	76	35	126
Portugal	**68**	**73**	**23**	**98**	**73**	**89**	**87**	**78**
Slovenia	**69**	**53**	**41**	**46**	**82**	**69**	**74**	**21**
Albania	70	83	88	47	94	24	102	118
Croatia	71	77	81	105	57	46	110	62
Japan	72	56	27	107	98	66	33	14
Malaysia	73	69	78	106	95	26	79	53
Lithuania	**74**	**66**	**42**	**138**	**39**	**63**	**42**	**22**
Uzbekistan	75	62	135	4	26	55	115	2
Armenia	76	67	74	133	105	16	40	67
Benin	77	58	7	77	109	114	66	7
Italy	**78**	**71**	**64**	**102**	**93**	**67**	**22**	**50**
Luxembourg	**79**	**99**	**59**	**109**	**62**	**37**	**139**	**116**
Mongolia	80	88	55	8	61	116	108	106
Romania	**81**	**78**	**79**	**123**	**70**	**59**	**98**	**27**
Cyprus	82	90	58	16	108	64	135	55
Uganda	83	70	112	12	10	122	91	30
Algeria	84	84	116	54	92	28	75	110
Latvia	**85**	**75**	**70**	**137**	**30**	**90**	**26**	**40**
Pakistan	86	72	69	94	118	42	61	24
Zambia	87	85	36	79	71	129	48	102
Kenya	88	79	89	85	51	115	72	39

Appendix Table 4. (Continued).

	smart	smart	smart	smart	smart	smart	smart	smart
	26 development index	26 development index, based on six dimensions	democracy	economic growth	gender	human development	R&D	social cohesion
Mexico	89	97	94	100	88	49	123	58
Egypt	90	89	117	43	113	20	109	77
Venezuela	91	94	109	127	60	45	96	79
Korea (Republic of)	92	96	85	58	114	53	125	9
Malta	**93**	**101**	**107**	**53**	**102**	**47**	**126**	**71**
Syria	94	103	129	44	100	29	114	109
Laos	95	68	119	25		44	80	5
Congo	96	126	71	96		95	39	
Uruguay	97	108	90	13	90	107	132	100
Paraguay	98	117	121	72	53	84	128	121
Czech Republic	**99**	**102**	**87**	**71**	**91**	**100**	**131**	**29**
Ukraine	100	93	102	136	63	75	44	34
Greece	**101**	**104**	**98**	**35**	**103**	**97**	**118**	**82**
Ethiopia	102	91	83	9	104	130	92	19
Singapore	103	100	110	130	107	51	58	47
Mauritania	104	115	111	40	86	110	113	119
Angola	105	127	101	68	43	132	68	
Mali	106	107	35	28	111	133	105	98
Djibouti	107	137	67	42		113	99	133
Yemen	108	98	96	19	122	68	69	89
Haiti	109	111	97	134		54	38	122
Myanmar	110	87	131	14		60	45	72

	smart	smart	smart	smart	smart	smart	smart	smart
	26 development index	26 development index, based on six dimensions	democracy	economic growth	gender	human development	R&D	social cohesion
Congo (Democratic Republic of the)	111	132	108	5		121	43	
Azerbaijan	112	95	132	2	110	94	84	95
Togo	113	133	75	128		103	47	
Iran	114	120	126	17	116	83	129	97
Saudi Arabia	115	114	128	78	121	36	100	64
Botswana	116	129	44	3	99	140	136	128
Nigeria	117	109	115	88	79	125	88	44
Cameroon	118	113	120	92	89	120	82	73
Rwanda	119	86	92	38		123	52	3
Turkey	120	121	113	117	119	73	117	91
Namibia	121	136	91	49	64	139	137	132
Guinea	122	106	103	61		117	90	28
Lebanon	123	131	134	10		101	71	
Estonia	**124**	**122**	**114**	**120**	**78**	**118**	**119**	**66**
Burkina Faso	125	116	104	26	106	137	120	12
Russia	126	112	130	124	75	108	29	46
Kazakhstan	127	118	138	73	46	112	111	52
Macedonia	128	134	127	70	101	111	133	127
Sierra Leone	129	128	63	74		135	49	129
Belarus	130	105	139	83	44	105	65	4
Hong Kong, China (SAR)	131	119	133	64		91	97	70
Burundi	132	110	95	110		126	56	15

Appendix Table 4. (Continued).

	smart	smart	smart	smart	smart	smart	smart	smart
	26 development index	26 development index, based on six dimensions	democracy	economic growth	gender	human development	R&D	social cohesion
Zimbabwe	133	125	118	140	77	134	73	65
Chad	134	123	125	60	117	131	112	1
Kuwait	135	138	137	31	115	99	138	
Niger	136	124	100	51		136	106	93
United Arab Emirates	137	130	136	56	120	82	140	105
Central African Republic,	138	135	105	87		138	104	130
Bosnia and Herzegovina	139	139	123	129		96	134	131
Sudan	140	140	140	7		127	121	

REFERENCES

Acemoglu, D. 2003. Cross-Country Inequality Trends. *Economic Journal,* (113): 121-149.

Acemoglu, D. 2005. Politics and Economics in Weak and Strong States. *Journal of Monetary Economics, Swiss National Bank,* Special Issue, (52): 1199-1226.

Acemoglu, D. 2009. *The Crisis of 2008: Structural Lessons for and from Economics.* As yet unpublished working paper, available from the website http://econ-www.mit.edu/faculty/acemoglu/other.

Acemoglu, D. 2010a. Theory, General Equilibrium, Political Economy and Empirics in Development Economics. *Journal of Economic Perspectives,* 24(2): 17-32.

Acemoglu, D. 2010b. When Does Labor Scarcity Encourage Innovation? *Journal of Political Economy,* 118(6): 1037-1078.

Acemoglu, D. and Dell, M. 2010. Productivity Differences Between and Within Countries. *American Economic Journal: Macroeconomics,* 2(1): 169–88.

Acemoglu, D. and Robinson, J. 2000. Why Did the West Extend the Franchise? Democracy, Inequality and Growth in Historical Perspective. *Quarterly Journal of Economics,* (115): 1167-1199.

Acemoglu, D. and Robinson, J. 2001. Inefficient Redistribution. *American Political Science Review*, (95): 649-61.

Acemoglu, D. and Robinson, J. 2006. Economic Backwardness in Political Perspective. *American Political Science Review,* 100: 115-131.

Acemoglu, D., Johnson, S. and Robinson, J. 2001. The Colonial Origins of Comparative Development: An Empirical Investigation. *American Economic Review,* (91): 1369-1401.

Acemoglu, D., Johnson, S. and Robinson, J. 2002. Reversal of Fortune: Geography and Institutions in the Making of the Modern World Income Distribution. *Quarterly Journal of Economics,* 117: 1231-1294.

Acemoglu, D., Johnson, S., and Robinson, J. 2005. The Rise of Europe: Atlantic Trade, Institutional Change and Growth. *American Economic Review,* June 2005, (95): 546-579.

Acemoglu, D., Johnson, S., Robinson, J., and Yared, P. 2008. Income and Democracy. *American Economic Review,* 98: 808-842.

Acosta, P., Calderon, C., Fajnzylber, P. et al. 2008. What is the impact of international remittances on poverty and inequality in Latin America? *World Development,* 36(1): 89-114.

Addison, T. and Heshmati, A. 2004. The new global determinants of FDI to developing countries. *Research in Banking and Finance,* 4, 151-186.

Afxentiou, P. C. 1990a. Basic Needs – As Survey of the Literature. *Revue Canadienne d'Etudes du Developpement – Canadian Journal of Development Studies,* 11(2): 241-257.

Afxentiou, P. C. 1990b. The Rhethoric and Substance of Basic Needs. *South African Journal of Economics,* 58(1): 78-87.

Aghion, Ph. and Howitt, P. 1992. A Model of Growth Through Creative Destruction. *Econometrica,* 60 (2), 323-351.

Agosin, M. and Machado, R. 2005. Foreign Investment in Developing Countries: Does it Crowd in Domestic Investment?. *Oxford Development Studies,* 33(2):149-162.

Alesina, A. and Perotti, R. 1994. The political economy of growth. A critical survey of the recent literature. *World Bank Economic Review,* 8(3): 351-371.

Alesina, A., Spolaore, E. and Wacziarg, R. 2000. Economic integration and political disintegration. *American Economic Review,* 90(5): 1276-1296.

Allsopp, C. and Artis, M. J. 2003. The assessment: EMU, four years on. *Oxford Review of Economic Policy,* 19(1): 1-29.

Amin, S. 1973. *Le developpement inegal. Essai sur les formations sociales du capitalisme peripherique'* [*Uneven development. Essay on the social formations of peripheral capitalism*] Paris: Editions de Minuit.

Amin, S. 1976. *Unequal Development: An Essay on the Social Formations of Peripheral Capitalism.* New York: Monthly Review Press.

Amin, S. 1980. The Class Structure of the Contemporary Imperialist System. *Monthly Review* 31(8): 9-26.

Amin, S. 1984. Was kommt nach der Neuen Internationalen Wirtschaftsordnung? Die Zukunft der Weltwirtschaft [What Comes After the New International Economic Order? The future of the world economy]. In *'Rote Markierungen International'* (Fischer H. and Jankowitsch P. (Eds.)), pp. 89 - 110, Vienna: Europaverlag.

Amin, S. 1989. *Eurocentrism. Translated by Russell Moore.* New York: Monthly Review Press.

Amin, S. 1992. *Empire of Chaos.* New York: Monthly Review Press.

Amin, S. 1994a. The Future of Global Polarization. *Review (Fernand Braudel Center, USA),* 17(3): 337-347.

Amin, S. 1994b. Die neue kapitalistische Globalisierung - die Herrschaft des Chaos [The new capitalist globalization - the rule of chaos]. *Starnberger Forschungsberichte*, 3(4), May: 7 - 26.

Amin, S. 1994c. *Re-reading the postwar period: an intellectual itinerary. Translated by Michael Wolfers.* New York: Monthly Review Press.

Amin, S. 1997a. *Capitalism in the Age of Globalization.* London, England: Zed Books.

Amin, S. 1997b. *Die Zukunft des Weltsystems. Herausforderungen der Globalisierung. Herausgegeben und aus dem Franzoesischen uebersetzt von Joachim Wilke* [*The future of the world system. Challenges of globalization. Edited and translated from the French by Joachim Wilke*]. Hamburg: VSA.

Amin, S., Arrighi, G., Frank A. G. and Wallerstein, I. 1982. *Dynamics of global crisis.* Basingstoke: Palgrave Macmillan.

Amuedo-Dorantes, C. and Pozo, S. 2004. Workers' remittances and the real exchange rate: A paradox of gifts. *World Development,* 32(8): 1407-1417.

Anand, S. and Ravallion, M. 1993. Human Development in Poor Countries. On the Role of Private Incomes and Public Services. *Journal of Economic Perspectives,* 7(1): 133-150.

Angelsen, A. and Kaimowitz, D. 1999. Rethinking the causes of deforestation: Lessons from economic models. *World Bank Research Observer,* 14(1): 73-98.

Anson, J. 1988. Mortality and Living Conditions. Relative Mortality Levels and their Relation to the Physical Quality of Life in Urban Populations. *Social Science & Medicine,* 27(9): 901-910.

Anson, J. 1991. Demographic Indexes as Social Indicators. *Environment and Planning.* 23(3): 433-446.

Arrighi, G. 1995. *The Long 20th Century. Money, Power, and the Origins of Our Times.* London, New York: Verso.

Auvinen, J. and Nafziger, E. W. 1999. The sources of humanitarian emergencies. *Journal of Conflict Resolution,* 43(3): 267-290.

Bandelji, N. 2009. The Global Economy as Instituted Process: The Case of Central and Eastern Europe. *American Sociological Review,* 74(1), 128-149, Feb 2009.

Barro, R. J. 1998. *Determinants of Economic Growth: A Cross-country Empirical Study.* Lionel Robbins Lectures. Cambridge, MA: MIT Press, first edition.

Barro, R. J. 2000. Inequality and growth in a panel of countries. *Journal of Economic Growth,* 5(1): 5-32.

Barro, R. J. 2003. Economic Growth in a Cross Section of Countries. *International Library of Critical Writings in Economics,* 159(1), 350-386.

Barro, R. J. 2004. Spirit of Capitalism Religion and Economic Development. *Harvard International Review,* vol. 25, no. 4, pp. 64-67.

Barro, R. J. 2006. Rare disasters and asset markets in the twentieth century. *The Quarterly Journal of Economics,* 121(3), 823-866.

Barro, R. J. 2012. *Convergence and Modernization Revisited.* Department of Economics, Harvard University.

Barro, R. J. and McCleary, R. M. 2003. Religion and Economic Growth across Countries. *American Sociological Review,* 68 (5): 760-781.

Barro, R. J. and Sala-i-Martin X. 1992. Convergence. *Journal of Political Economy.* 100 (2): 223-251.

Barro, R. J. and Sala-i-Martin, X. 2003. *Economic Growth.* Cambridge, MA: MIT Press, Second edition.

Barro, R. J. and Ursúa, J. F. 2008. Macroeconomic Crises since 1870. *Brookings Papers on Economic Activity,* Spring, pp. 255-335. Available at: http://www.people.fas.harvard.edu/~jfursua/papers/bpea.pdf.

Barro, R. J. and Ursua, R. F. 2011. *Barro-Ursua Macroeconomic Data.* Available at: https://scholar.harvard.edu/barro/publications/barro-ursua-macroeconomic-data.

Barro, R. J., Ursua, J. F. and Weng, J. 2020. The Coronavirus and the Great Influenza Epidemic - Lessons from the 'Spanish Flu' for the Coronavirus's Potential Effects on Mortality and Economic Activity 2020). *CESifo Working Paper No. 8166.* Available at SSRN: https://ssrn.com/abstract=3556305.

Beer, L. 1999. Income Inequality and Transnational Corporate Penetration. *Journal of World Systems Research,* 5 (1), 1 – 25.

Bekaert, G., Harvey, C. R., and Lundblad, C. 2005. Does financial liberalization spur growth? *Journal of Financial Economics,* 77 (1), pp. 3-55.

Biswas, B. and Ram, R. 1986. Military Expenditures and Economic Growth in Less-Developed Countries. An Augmented Model and Further Evidence. *Economic Development and Cultural Change,* 34(2): 361-372.

Blankenau, W. F. and Simpson, N. B. 2004. Public education expenditures and growth. *Journal of Development Economics,* 73(2): 583-605.

Bobróvnikov, A. V. 2004. *Makrocikly v ekonomike stran Latinskoj Ameriki.* [*Macorcycles in the economies of Latin American countries*]. Moskva: Inst. Latinskoj Ameriki.

Bornschier, V. 1976., *Wachstum, Konzentration und Multinationalisierung von Industrieunternehmen [Growth, concentration and multinationalization of industrial companies*]. Frauenfeld; Stuttgart: Huber.

Bornschier, V. 1980. Multinational corporations and economic growth: A cross-national test of the decapitalization thesis. *Journal of Development Economics,* 7(2), 191-210.

Bornschier, V. 1980a. Multinational Corporations, Economic Policy and National Development in the World System. *International Social Science Journal,* 32 (1), 158-172.

Bornschier, V. 1980b. *Multinationale Konzerne, Wirtschaftspolitik und nationale Entwicklung im Weltsystem. Mit Beiträgen von Thanh-Huyen Ballmer-Cao* [*et al.*]. [Multinational corporations, economic policy and national development in the world system. With contributions by Thanh-Huyen Ballmer-Cao [et al.] Frankfurt/Main; New York: Campus.

Bornschier, V. 1981. Dependent Industrialization in the World Economy: Some Comments and Results concerning a Recent Debate. *The Journal of Conflict Resolution,* 25 (3), 371-400.

Bornschier, V. 1982. The World Economy in the World System. Structure Dependence and Change. *International Social Science Journal,* 34 (1), 38-59.

Bornschier, V. 1983. World economy, level development and income distribution: An integration of different approaches to the explanation of income inequality. *World Development*, 11(1), 11-20.

Bornschier, V. 1983. World economy, level development and income distribution: An integration of different approaches to the explanation of income inequality. *World Development,* 11 (1), 11-20.

Bornschier, V. 1996. *Western society in transition.* New Brunswick, N.J.: Transaction Publishers.

Bornschier, V. 2002. Changing Income Inequality in the Second Half of the 20th Century: Preliminary Findings and Propositions for Explanations' *Journal of World-Systems Research,* available at: http://jwsr.ucr.edu/ index.phpVIII, 1, Winter: 100 – 127.

Bornschier, V. and Ballmer-Cao, T. H. 1978. *Multinational corporations in the world economy and national development: an empirical study of income per capita growth 1960-1975.* Department of Sociology, University of Zurich, Switzerland.

Bornschier, V. and Ballmer-Cao, T. H. 1979. Income inequality: a cross-national study of the relationships between MNC-penetration, dimensions of the power structure and income distribution. *American Sociological Review,* 487-506.

Bornschier, V. and Ballmer-Cao, T. H. 1979. Income Inequality: A Cross-National Study of the Relationships Between MNC-Penetration, Dimensions of the Power Structure and Income Distribution. *American Sociological Review,* 44 (3), 438-506.

Bornschier, V. and Chase-Dunn, Ch. K. 1985. *Transnational Corporations and Underdevelopment.* N. Y., N. Y.: Praeger.

Bornschier, V., Chase-Dunn, Ch. K., Rubinson, R 1978. Cross-National Evidence of the Effects of Foreign Investment and Aid on Economic Growth and Inequality: A Survey of Findings and a Reanalysis. *American Journal of Sociology,* 84 (3), 651-683.

Bovenberg, A. L. and van Ewijk, C. 1997. Progressive taxes, equity, and human capital accumulation in an endogenous growth model with overlapping generations. *Journal of Public Economics,* 64(2): 153-179.

Brand, U. 2005. *Gegen-Hegemonie. Perspektiven globalisierungskritischer Strategien* [*Counter-hegemony. Perspectives of strategies critical of globalization*]. Hamburg: VSA.

Brand, U. and Goerg, Ch. 2003. *Postfordistische Naturverhältnisse: Konflikte um genetische Ressourcen und die Internationalisierung des Staates* [*Post-Fordist relationships of nature: conflicts over genetic resources and the internationalization of the state*]. Muenster: Westfaelisches Dampfboot.

Brand, U. and Raza, W. (Eds.) 2003. *Fit für den Postfordismus?: theoretisch-politische Perspektiven des Regulationsansatzes* [*Fit for Post-Fordism ?: Theoretical-political perspectives of the regulatory approach*]. Muenster: Westfaelisches Dampfboot.

Brand, U. et al. (Eds.) 2001. *Nichtregierungsorganisationen in der Transformation des Staates* [*Non-governmental organizations in the transformation of the state*]. Muenster: Westfaelisches Dampfboot.

Brand, U. et al. 2000. *Global governance: Alternative zur neoliberalen Globalisierung?* [*Global governance: an alternative to neoliberal globalization?*] Muenster: Westfaelisches Dampfboot.

Brand, U. et al. 2008. *Conflicts in environmental regulation and the internationalisation of the state: contested terrains.* London: Routledge.

Burckett, P. 1999. *Marx and nature: A red and green perspective.* New York: St. Martin's Press.

Buti, F., Franco, D., and Ongena, H. 1998. Fiscal discipline and flexibility in EMU: The implementation of the stability and growth pact. *Oxford Review of Economic Policy,* 14(3): 81-97.

Cardoso, F. H. 1977. El Consumo de la Teoría de la Dependencia en los Estados Unidos [The Consumption of Dependency Theory in the United States] *El Trimestre Economico,* 173, 44, 1, 33 - 52.

Cardoso, F. H. 1979. *Development under Fire.* Mexico D. F.: Instituto Latinoamericano de Estudios Transnacionales, DEE/D/24 i, Mayo (Mexico 20 D. F., Apartado 85 - 025.

Cardoso, F. H. and Faletto, E. 1971. *Dependencia y desarrollo en América Latina* [*Dependency and development in Latin America*]. Mexico D. F.: Editorial Siglo I.

Carruthers J. I. And Ulfarsson, G. 2007. Does 'smart growth' matter to public finance? *Urban Studies,* 45(9): 1791-1823.

CEPAL/ECLAC 2002. *Globalización y desarrollo* [*Globalization and development*]. United Nations Economic Commission for Latin America (Santiago de Chile), available at http://www.eclac.cl/cgi-bin/getProd.asp?xml=/publicaciones/xml/6/10026/P10026.xml&xsl=/tpl/p9f.xsl&base=/MDG/tpl/top-bottom. xsl.

Chase-Dunn, Ch. K. 1975. The Effects of International Economic Dependence on Development and Inequality: a Cross- national Study. *American Sociological Review,* 40 (4), 720 - 738.

Chen, X. M. 1995. The evolution of free economic zones and the recent development of cross-national growth zones. *International Journal of Urban and Regional Research,* 19(4): 593-616.

Cheng W. Y. 1989. Testing the Food-First Hypothesis. A Cross-national Study of Dependency, Sectoral Growth and Food-Intake in Less Developed Countries. *World Development,* 17(1): 17-27.

Clauß, G. and Ebner, H. 1970. *Grundlagen der Statistik für Psychologen, Pädagogen und Soziologen* [*Basics of statistics for psychologists, educators and sociologists*]. Volk und Wissen Volkseigener Verlag.

Coleman, J. S. 1965. *Education and Political Development.* Princeton: Princeton University Press.

Constant, A., Gataullina, L., Zimmermann, K. F. and Zimmermann, L. 2006. *Clash of Cultures: Muslims and Christians in the Ethnosizing Process.* German Institute for Economic Research, Discussion Paper 628, Berlin, October 2006, available at: http://ideas.repec.org/p/diw/diwwpp/dp628.html.

Cook, C. J. 1995. Savings rates and income distribution. Further evidence from LDCs. *Applied Economics,* 27(1): 71-82.

Cornia, G. A. 2019. *A theory of why potentially favourable political and economic changes may lead to mortality crises* (No. wp2019_23. rdf). Universita'degli Studi di Firenze, Dipartimento di Scienze per l'Economia e l'Impresa.

Cornia, G. A. and Paniccià, R. 2000. *The mortality crisis in transitional economies.* OUP Oxford.

Crenshaw, E. and Robison, K. 2010. Socio-Demographic Determinants of Economic Growth: Age-Structure, Preindustrial Heritage and Sociolinguistic Integration. *Social Forces,* 88(5): 2217-2240.

Cropper, M. L. and Oates, W. E. 1992. Environmental Economics – A Survey. *Journal of Economic Literature,* 30, 2: 675-740.

D'Elia, E. 2020. Reforming Europe's fiscal rules. *Social Europe*, March, 24, 2020 available at https://www.socialeurope.eu/reforming-europes-fiscal-rules.

De Haan, J; Lundstrom, S; Sturm, J. E. 2006. Market oriented institutions and policies and economic growth: a critical survey. *Journal of Economic Surveys,* 20(2): 157-191.

de la Porte, C., Pochet, P., and Room, G. 2001. Social benchmarking, policy making and new governance in the EU. *Journal of European Social Policy,* 11(4): 291-307.

De Soysa I. and Oneal J. R. 1999. 'Boon or Bane? – Reassessing the Productivity of Foreign Direct Investment.' *American Sociological Review,* 64:766–782.

De Soysa, I. and Ragnhild, N. Islam's bloody innards? Religion and political terror, 1980-2000. *International Studies Quarterly,* 51(4): 927-943.

D'Elia, E. and De Santis, R. (2019). *Growth divergence and income inequality in OECD countries: The role of trade and financial openness.* LEQS Paper, (148), available at SSRN: https://ssrn.com/abstract=3489127.

Devezas, T. C. (Ed.) 2006. Kondratieff waves, warfare and world security: *[Proceedings of the NATO Advanced Research Workshop on The Influence of Chance Events and Socioeconomic Long Waves in the New Arena of Asymmetric Warfare,* Covilhã, Portugal, 14 - 18 February 2005]. Amsterdam: IOS Press.

Devezas, T. C. and Corredine, J. T. 2001. The biological determinants of long-wave behavior in socioeconomic growth and development. *Technological Forecasting and Social Change,* 68 (1), 1-57.

Dick, Ch. and Jorgenson, A. K. 2010. Sectoral Foreign Investment and Nitrous Oxide Emissions: A Quantitative Investigation. *Society and Natural Resources,* 23(1), 71-82.

Dietz, T., Rosa, E. A., York, R. 2007. Driving the human ecological footprint. *Frontiers in Ecology and the Environment,* 5(1): 13-18.

Dietz, T., Rosa, E. A., York, R. 2009. Environmentally Efficient Well-Being: Rethinking Sustainability as the Relationship between Human Well-being and Environmental Impact. *Human Ecology Review,* 16, (1): 114-123.

Dinopoulos, E. And Thompson, P. 1999. Scale effects in Schumpeterian models of economic growth. *Journal of Evolutionary Economics,* 9(2): 157-185.

Dixon, W. J. 1987. Progress in the Provision of Basic Human Needs. Latin America, 1960-1980. *Journal of Developing Areas,* 21(2): 129-140.

Dixon, W. J. and Boswell T. 1996a. 'Dependency, Disarticulation, and Denominator Effects: Another Look at Foreign Capital Penetration.' *American Journal of Sociology,* 102 (2), 543–562.

Dixon, W. J. and Boswell T. 1996b. 'Differential Productivity, Negative Externalities, and Foreign Capital Dependency: Reply to Firebaugh.' *American Journal of Sociology,* 102 (2), 576–584.

Dixon, W. J. and Moon, B. E. 1986. The Military Burden and Basic Human Needs. *Journal of Conflict Resolution,* 30(4): 660-684.

Dixon, W. J. and Moon, B. E. 1989. Domestic Political Conflict and Basic Needs Outcomes. An Empirical Assessment. *Comparative Political Studies,* 22(2): 178-198.

Dollar, D. 1992a. Growth is good for the poor. *Journal of Economic Growth,* 7(3): 195-225.

Dollar, D. 1992b. Outward-oriented developing countries really do grow more rapidly. Evidence from 95 LDCs, 1976-1985. *Economic Development and Cultural Change,* 40(3): 523-544.

Doucouliagos, H. and Paldam, M. 2008. Aid effectiveness on growth: A meta study. *European Journal of Political Economy,* 24(1): 1-24.

Downs, A. 2005. Smart growth - why we discuss it more than we do it. *Journal of the American Planning Association,* 71(4): 367-378.

Durlauf, St. N., Kourtellos, A. and Tan, Ch. M. 2008. Are any Growth Theories Robust? *The Economic Journal,* 118(1), 329-346.

Dutt, A. K. 1997. The pattern of direct foreign investment and economic growth. *World Development,* 25 (11), 1925-1936.

Easterlin, R. A. 1995. Will raising the incomes of all increase the happiness of all? *Journal of Economic Behavior & Organization,* 27(1): 35-47.

Easterlin, R. A. 2001. Income and happiness: Towards a unified theory. *Economic Journal,* 111(473): 465-484.

Easterly, W. 2000. The *Middle Class Consensus and Economic Development.* (May 2000. World Bank Policy Research Working Paper No. 2346. Available at SSRN: http://ssrn.com/abstract=630718 (Data available at http://www.cgdev.org/doc/expert%20pages/easterly/easterly_consensusdata.xls in EXCEL-format. The data are also still retrievable by a Google search, using the search profile words easterly_consensusdata. xls).

Easterly, W. 2002. *Inequality does Cause Underdevelopment: New evidence.* Center for Global Development, Working Paper 1, January 2002, available at: http://www.cgdev.org/wp/cgd_wp001_rev.pdf.

Easterly, W. and Levine, R. 1997. Africas Growth Tragedy: Policies and Ethnic Divisions. *Quarterly Journal of Economics,* 112(4), 1203-1250.

Easterly, W. and Schmidthebbel, K. 1993. Fiscal deficits and macroeconomic performance in developing countries. *World Bank Research Observer,* 8(2): 211-237.

Edwards, S. 1993. Openness, trade liberalization, and growth in developing countries. *Journal of Economic Literature,* 31(3): 1358-1393.

Egert, B; Drine I; Lommatzsch K; et al. 2003. The Balassa-Samuelson effect in Central and Eastern Europe: myth or reality? *Journal of Comparative Economics,* 31(3): 552-572.

Ehrhardt-Martinez, K., Crenshaw, E. M., Jenkins, J. C. 2002. Deforestation and the Environmental Kuznets Curve: A Cross-National Investigation of Intervening Mechanisms. *Social Science Quarterly,* vol. 83(1), 226-243, Mar 2002.

Fain, H. D. et al. 1997. World-System Position, Tropical Climate, National Development, and Infant Mortality: A Cross-National Analysis of 86 Countries. *Human Ecology Review,* 3: 197-203.

Farhani, S., Mrizak, S., Chaibi, A., Rault, C. (2014). The environmental Kuznets curve and sustainability: A panel data analysis. *Energy Policy,* 71, pp. 189-198. doi: 10.1016/j.enpol.2014.04.030.

Faria, J. R; Leon-Ledesma, M. 2003. Testing the Balassa-Samuelson effect: Implications for growth and the PPP. *Journal of Macroeconomics,* 25(2): 241-253.

Feldstein, M. 1994. Fiscal policies, capital formation, and capitalism. *European Economic Review,* 39(3-4): 399-420.

Firebaugh, G. 1992. 'Growth Effects of Foreign and Domestic Investment.' *American Journal of Sociology,* 98:105–130.

Firebaugh, G. and Beck, F. D. 1994. 'Does Economic Growth Benefit the Masses? Growth, Dependence, and Welfare in the Third World.' *American Sociological Review,* 59, 631–653.

Fosu, A. K. 2009. Inequality and the Impact of Growth on Poverty: Comparative Evidence for Sub-Saharan Africa. *Journal of Development Studies,* 45(5): 726-745.

Fosu, A. K. 2010a. The Effect of Income Distribution on the Ability of Growth to Reduce Poverty: Evidence from Rural and Urban African Economies. *American Journal of Economics and Sociology,* 69(3): 1034-1053.

Fosu, A. K. 2010b. Does inequality constrain poverty reduction programs? Evidence from Africa. *Journal of Policy Modeling,* 32(6): 818-827.

Fosu, A. K. 2010c). Inequality, Income, and Poverty: Comparative Global Evidence. *Social Science Quarterly,* 91(5): 1432-1446.

Frank, A. G. 1967. *Capitalism and underdevelopment in Latin America: historical studies of Chile and Brazil.* New York: Monthly Review Press.

Frank, A. G. 1998. *ReOrient: Global Economy in the Asian Age.* Ewing, USA: University of California Press.

Frankel, J. A. and Romer D. 1999. Does Trade Cause Growth? *American Economic Review,* 89(3), 379-99.

Frankel, J. A., Romer, D. 1999. Does trade cause growth? *American Economic Review,* 89(3): 379-399.

Freedom House (2018). *Freedom in the World,* 2018. Available at https://freedomhouse.org/report/freedom-world/freedom-world-2018.

Frey, B. S. and Stutzer, A. 2002. What can economists learn from happiness research? *Journal of Economic Literature,* 40(2): 402-435.

Froebel, F. et al. 1980. *The new international division of labour: structural unemployment in industrialised countries and industrialisation in developing countries.* Cambridge; New York: Cambridge University Press; Paris: Editions de la Maison des Sciences de lHomme, 1980.

Fukuyama, F. 1995. *Trust: The social virtues and the creation of prosperity* (No. D10 301 c. 1/c. 2). New York: Free press.

Fukuyama, F. 2006. *The end of history and the last man.* Simon and Schuster.

Furman, J. L., Porter, M. E., and Stern, S. 2002. The determinants of national innovative capacity. *Research Policy,* 31 (6), pp. 899-933.

Furtado, C. 1963. *The economic growth of Brazil: a survey from colonial to modern times.* Translated by Ricardo W. de Aguiar and Eric Charles Drysdale. Berkeley: University of California Press.

Furtado, C. 1964. *Development and underdevelopment.* Trans. by R. W. de Aguiar and E. C. Drysdale. Berkeley: California University Press.

Furtado, C. 1976. *Economic development of Latin America: historical background and contemporary problems.* Translated by Suzette Macedo. Cambridge; New York: Cambridge University Press.

Furtado, C. 1983. *Accumulation and development: the logic of industrial civilization.* Translated by Suzette Macedo. Oxford: M. Robertson.

Gallup, J. L. and Sachs, J. D. with Mellinger, A. D. 1999. Geography and Economic Development, In *Annual World Bank Conference on Development Economics 1998,* Boris Pleskovic and Joseph E. Stiglitz, eds. Washington, DC: The World Bank (April). Also published in *International Regional Science Review* 22 (2), 179-232.

Galtung, J. 1971. A Structural Theory of Imperialism. *Journal of Peace Research,* 8 (2), 81 - 117.

Gine, X. and Townsend, R. M. 2004. Evaluation of financial liberalization: a general equilibrium model with constrained occupation choice. *Journal of Development Economics,* 74(2): 269-307.

Glomm, G. and Ravikumar, B. 1997. Productive government expenditures and long-run growth. *Journal of Economic Dynamics & Control,* 21(1): 183-204.

Goldstein, J. S. 1985. Basic Human Needs – The Plateau Curve. *World Development,* 13(5), 595-609.

Goldstein, J. S. 1988. *Long Cycles: Prosperity and War in the Modern Age* New Haven: Yale University Press.

Gould, E. D. 2002. Rising wage inequality, comparative advantage, and the growing importance of general skills in the United States. *Journal of Labor Economics,* 20(1): 105-147.

Grier, K. B. and Tullock, G. 1989. An empirical analysis of cross-national economic growth. *Journal of Monetary Economics,* 24(2), 259–76.

Grinin, L., Tausch, A. and Korotayev, A. 2016. *Economic cycles, crises, and the global periphery.* Cham, Sitzerland: Springer.

Guger A., Marterbauer M. and Walterskirchen, E. 2006. Growth Policy in the Spirit of Steindl and Kalecki. *Metroeconomica,* 57(3), 428–442.

Guger A., Marterbauer M. and Walterskirchen, E. 2006. Zur Aktualität der Politischen Ökonomie von Josef Steindl [On the topicality of political economy by Josef Steindl]. *Kurswechsel,* 4/2006, 18-26, available at http://ewald.walterskirchen.wifo.ac.at/.

Guger, A., Marterbauer, M., and Walterskirchen, E. 2004. *Growth Policy in the Spirit of Steindl and Kalecki.* WIFO Working papers, 240, 2004, available at: http://ewald.walterskirchen.wifo.ac.at/.

Gwartney, J. D., Lawson, R. A. and Holcombe, R. G. 1999. Economic freedom and the environment for growth. *Journal of Institutional and Theoretical Economics – Zeitschrift fuer die Gesamte Staatswissenschaft,* 155(4): 643-663.

Gygli, S., Haelg, F., Niklas Potrafke, N. and Sturm, J. E. 2019. The KOF Globalisation Index – Revisited, *Review of International Organizations,* 14(3), 543-574, https://doi.org/10.1007/s11558-019-09344-2.

Halal, W. E. 1988. The New Capitalism. *Futurist,* 22(1): 26-32.

Hall, R. E. and Jones, Ch. I. 1999. Why Do Some Countries Produce so Much More Output per Worker than Others? *Quarterly Journal of Economics,* 114(1), 83-116.

Hamid, A. 2007. Military Expenditures and Inequality: Empirical Evidence from Global Data. *Defence and Peace Economics,* 2007. 18(6), December, pp. 519–535.

Hatton, T. J. and Williamson, J. A. 2009. *Vanishing Third World Emigrants?* Harvard University, Department of Economics, available at:

http://www.economics.harvard.edu/faculty/williamson/jwilliam workingpapers.

Hayek, F. A. 1945. The Use of Knowledge in Society. *American Economic Review,* 35, 4: 519-530.

Hayek, F. A. 1960. *The constitution of liberty.* Chicago: University of Chicago Press.

Hayek, F. A. 1980. *Individualism and economic order.* University of Chicago Press.

Hayek, F. A. 1989. *The collected works of F. A. Hayek/edited by W. W. Bartley III.* Chicago, Ill.: University of Chicago Press.

Hayek, F. A. 1998. *The Fatal Conceit: The Errors of Socialism.* London and New York: Routledge.

Hayek, F. A. 2012. *Law, legislation and liberty: A new statement of the liberal principles of justice and political economy.* Routledge.

Haynes, J. 2001. Transnational religious actors and international politics. *Third World Quarterly,* 22(2): 143-158.

Heintz, P. 1972. *A macrosociological theory of societal systems; with special reference to the international system.* Bern: H. Huber.

Helliwell, J. F. 1994. Empirical linkages between democracy and economic growth. *British Journal of Political Science,* 24(April): 225-248.

Heo, U. 1998. Modeling the defense-growth relationship around the globe. *Journal of Conflict Resolution,* 42(5): 637-657.

Herkenrath, M. 2003. *Transnationale Konzerne im Weltsystem. Globale Unternehmen, nationale Wirtschaftspolitik und das Problem nachholender Entwicklung* [*Transnational corporations in the world system. Global corporations, national economic policies and the problem of catching up development*]. Wiesbaden: Westdeutscher Verlag.

Herkenrath, M. and Bornschier, V. 2003. Transnational Corporations in World Development – Still the Same Harmful Effects in an Increasingly Globalized World Economy? *Journal of world-systems research,* ix(1), winter 2003, 105–139, http://jwsr.ucr.edu, issn 1076–156x.

Herkenrath, M., Koenig C., Scholtz, H. and Volken, Th. 2005. Convergence and Divergence in the Contemporary World System: An Introduction. *International Journal of Comparative Sociology,* vol. 46(5-6), 363-382.

Hertz, E., Hebert, J. R., Landon, J. 1994. Social and environmental factors and life expectancy, infant mortality and maternal mortality rates. Results of a cross-national comparison. *Social Science & Medicine,* 39(1): 105-114.

Heshmati, A. 2006a. Measurement of a Multidimensional Index of Globalization. *Global Economy Journal*, 6 (2), Paper 1.

Heshmati, A. 2006b. The World Distribution of Income and Income Inequality: A Review of the Economic Literature', *Journal of World Systems Research,* 12 (1), 61-107.

Heshmati, A. 2007. *Global Trends in Income Inequality.* Hauppauge, New York: Nova Science Publishers.

Heshmati, A. and Tausch, A. (Eds.) 2007. *Roadmap to Bangalore? Globalization, the EU's Lisbon process and the structures of global inequality.* Haupauge, New York, NY: Nova Science Publishing.

Holmberg, S., Rothstein, B., Nasiritousi, N. 2009. Quality of Government: What You Get. *Annual Review of Political Science,* 12: 135-161.

Huntington, S. P. 1968. *Political order in changing societies.* New Haven: Yale University Press.

Huntington, S. P. 1996. *The clash of civilizations and the remaking of world order.* New York: Simon & Schuster.

IBM SPSS 2007. *Statistical Package for the Social Sciences, User Guide.* Version 14, August 2007.

IBM SPSS 2011. *IBM-SPSS Statistics 20 Algorithms.* Armonk, New York. (URL: http://www-01.ibm.com/support/docview.wss?uid=swg 27021213#en).

IMF 2009. *World Economic Outlook database* available at: http://www.imf.org/external/pubs/ft/weo/2009/01/weodata/download.aspx.

Johnson, N. P. and Mueller, J. 2002. Updating the accounts: global mortality of the 1918-1920" Spanish" influenza pandemic. *Bulletin of the History of Medicine,* 105-115.

Jorgenson, A. K. 2003. Consumption and Environmental Degradation: A Cross-National Analysis of the Ecological Footprint. *Social Problems,* Vol. 50(3), 374-394.

Jorgenson, A. K. 2004. Global Inequality, Water Pollution, and Infant Mortality. *The Social Science Journal,* 41(2), 279-288.

Jorgenson, A. K. 2004. Uneven Processes and Environmental Degradation in the World-Economy. *Human Ecology Review,* 11(2), 103-117.

Jorgenson, A. K. 2005. Unpacking International Power and the Ecological Footprints of Nations: A Quantitative Cross-National Study. *Sociological Perspectives,* 48(3), 383-402.

Jorgenson, A. K. 2006. Global Warming and the Neglected Greenhouse Gas: A Cross-National Study of the Social Causes of Methane Emissions Intensity, 1995. *Social Forces,* 84(3), 1779-1798.

Jorgenson, A. K. 2006. Unequal Ecological Exchange and Environmental Degradation: A Theoretical Proposition and Cross-National Study of Deforestation, 1990-2000. *Rural Sociology,* 71(4), 685-712.

Jorgenson, A. K. 2007. Does foreign investment harm the air we breathe and the water we drink? A cross-national study of carbon dioxide emissions and organic water pollution in less-developed countries, 1975 to 2000. *Organization & Environment,* 20(2), 135-157.

Jorgenson, A. K. 2007. Foreign Direct Investment and Pesticide Use Intensity in Less-Developed Countries: A Quantitative Investigation. *Society and Natural Resources,* 20(1), 73-83.

Jorgenson, A. K. 2008. Structural Integration and the Trees: An Analysis of Deforestation in Less-Developed Countries, 1990-2005. *The Sociological Quarterly,* 49(3), 503-527, Summer 2008.

Jorgenson, A. K. 2009. Foreign Direct Investment and the Environment, the Mitigating Influence of Institutional and Civil Society Factors, and Relationships between Industrial Pollution and Human Health. *Organization & Environment,* 22(2), 135-157.

Jorgenson, A. K. 2009. Political-Economic Integration, Industrial Pollution and Human Health A Panel Study of Less-Developed Countries, 1980-2000. *International Sociology,* 24(1), 115-143.

Jorgenson, A. K. 2009. The Sociology of Unequal Exchange in Ecological Context: A Panel Study of Lower-Income Countries, 1975-2000. *Sociological Forum,* 24(1), 22-46.

Jorgenson, A. K. 2009. The Transnational Organization of Production, the Scale of Degradation, and Ecoefficiency: A Study of Carbon Dioxide Emissions in Less-Developed Countries. *Human Ecology Review,* 16(1), 64-74.

Jorgenson, A. K. and Burns, T. J. 2007. The political-economic causes of change in the ecological footprints of nations, 1991-2001: A quantitative investigation. *Social Science Research,* 36(2), 834-853.

Jorgenson, A. K. and Burns, Th. J. 2004. Globalization, the Environment, and Infant Mortality: A Cross National Study. *Humboldt Journal of Social Relations,* 28(1), 7-52.

Jorgenson, A. K. and Clark, B. 2009. The Economy, Military, and Ecologically Unequal Exchange Relationships in Comparative Perspective: A Panel Study of the Ecological Footprints of Nations, 1975-2000. *Social Problems,* 56(4), 621-646.

Jorgenson, A. K. and Kuykendall, K. A. 2008. Globalization, Foreign Investment Dependence and Agriculture Production: Pesticide and Fertilizer Use in Less-developed Countries, 1990-2000. *Social Forces,* 87(1), 529-560.

Jorgenson, A. K., and Burns, T. J. 2004. Globalization, the Environment, and Infant Mortality: A Cross National Study. *Humboldt Journal of Social Relations,* 28(1), 7-52.

Jorgenson, A. K., Austin, K. and Dick, Ch. 2009. Ecologically Unequal Exchange and the Resource Consumption/Environmental Degradation Paradox. *International Journal of Comparative Sociology,* 50(3-4), 263-284.

Jorgenson, A. K., Dick, C., and Mahutga, M. C. 2007. Foreign investment dependence and the environment: An ecostructural approach. *Social Problems,* 54(3), 371-394.

Kakwani, N. 1993. Performance in Living Standards. An International Comparison. *Journal of Development Economics,* 41(2): 307-336.

Kakwani, N. 1995. Structural Adjustment and Performance in Living Standards in Developing Countries. *Development and Change,* 26(3): 469-502.

Kalecki, M. 1943. Political aspects of full employment. *Political Quarterly,* 14 (4), pp. 322–331.

Kalecki, M. 1966. *Studies in the theory of business cycles, 1933-1939.* New York, A. M. Kelley.

Kalecki, M. 1968. *Theory of economic dynamics; an essay on cyclical and long-run changes in capitalist economy.* New York: Monthly Review Press.

Kalecki, M. 1968. Trend and business cycle reconsidered. *The Economic Journal,* 78 (310), pp. 263–276.

Kalecki, M. 1971. *Selected essays on the dynamics of the capitalist economy 1933-1970*. CUP Archive.

Kalecki, M. 1971. *Selected essays on the dynamics of the capitalist economy 1933-1970.* Cambridge [Eng.]: Cambridge University Press.

Kalecki, M. 1979. *Essays on Developing Economies. With an Introduction by Professor Joan Robinson.* Hassocks, Sussex: The Harvester Press.

Kalecki, M. 1996. The maintenance of full employment after the transition period: A comparison of the problem in the United States and United Kingdom (Reprinted from International Labour Review, vol 52, 1945), *International Labour Review,* 135(3-4), 359-365.

Kalecki, M. and Feiwel, G. R. 1972. *The last phase in the transformation of capitalism.* New York: Monthly Review Press.

Kamarck, A. M. 1976. *The Tropics and Economic Development: A Provocative Inquiry into the Poverty of Nations.* Baltimore: Johns Hopkins.

Kearney, A. T., Inc., and the Carnegie Endowment for International Peace 2002. Globalizations Last Hurrah?' *Foreign Policy,* January/February: 38-51.

Kearney, A. T., Inc., and the Carnegie Endowment for International Peace 2003. Measuring Globalization: Whos up, whos down?' *Foreign Policy,* January/February: 60-72.

Kentor J. 1998. 'The Long-Term Effects of Foreign Investment Dependence on Economic Growth 1940–1990.' *American Journal of Sociology,* 103 (4), 1024–1046.

Kentor J. and Boswell T. 2003. 'Foreign Capital Dependence and Development: A New Direction.' *American Sociological Review,* 68 (2):301-313.

Kentor, J. 1998. The Long-Term Effects of Foreign Investment Dependence on Economic Growth, 1940-1990. *The American Journal of Sociology,* 103 (4), 1024-1046.

Kerbo, H. 2005a. 'Foreign Investment and Disparities in Economic Development and Poverty Reduction: A Comparative-Historical Analysis of the Buddhist Countries of Southeast Asia.' *International Journal of Comparative Sociology,* 46, 425-459.

Kerbo, H. 2005b. *World Poverty: The Roots of Global Inequality and the Modern World System.* New York: McGraw-Hill.

Khan, H. 1991. Measurement and Determinants of Socioeconomic Development. *Social Indicators Research,* 24(2): 153-175.

King, L. A. 1998. Economic growth and basic human needs. *International Studies Quarterly,* 42(2): 385-400.

Klitgaard, R. and Fedderke, J. 1995. Social integration and disintegration: An exploratory analysis of cross-country data. *World Development,* 23 (3), 357-369.

Knight, K. W. and Rosa E. A. 2011. The environmental efficiency of well-being: A cross-national analysis. *Social Science Research,* 40(3): 931-949.

Kohler, G. and Tausch, A. 2001. *'Global Keynesianism: unequal exchange and global exploitation'* Huntington, N. Y.: Nova Science Publishers.

Kohr, L. 1957. *The breakdown of nations.* New York, Rinehart.

Kohr, L. 1958. The Velocity Theory of Population. *Land Economics,* 34(2), 178-181.

Kohr, L. 1960. The History of the Common Market. *The Journal of Economic History,* Vol. 20(3): 441-454.

Kohr, L. 1977. *The overdeveloped nations: the diseconomies of scale.* New York: Schocken Books.

Kohr, L. 1992. Leopold Kohr on the Desirable Scale of States. *Population and Development Review,* Vol. 18(4): 745-750.

Kormendi, R. C. and Meguire, P. 1985. Macroeconomic determinants of growth: Crosscountry evidence. *Journal of Monetary Economics,* 16(2), 141–63.

Korotayev, A. V. and Tsirel, S. V. 2010. A Spectral Analysis of World GDP Dynamics: Kondratieff Waves, Kuznets Swings, Juglar and Kitchin Cycles in Global Economic Development, and the 2008–2009 *Economic Crisis. Structure and Dynamics,* 4(1), Retrieved from: http://www.escholarship.org/uc/item/9jv108xp

Krasilshchikov, V. 2008. *The Rise and Decline of Catching Up Development. An Experience of Russia and Latin America with Implications for Asian Tigers.* Entelequia, Revista Interdisciplinar, e-books, Málaga, available from Internet: http://www.eumed.net/entelequia/en.lib.php?a=b008.

Kuznets, S. 1940. Schumpeters Business Cycles. *The American Economic Review,* 30 (2) 157 - 69.

Kuznets, S. 1955. Economic Growth and Income Inequality. *American Economic Review,* 45, 1: 1-28.

Kuznets, S. 1976. *Modern Economic Growth: Rate, Structure and Spread.* New Haven, CT: Yale University Press.

La Porta, R., Lopez de Silanes, F., Shlejfer A. et al. 1999. The quality of government. *Journal of Law, Economics and Organization,* 15(1): 222-279.

Łaski K. and Podkaminer L. 2014. Net Private Savings in Relation to the Government's Financial Balance. In: Bellofiore R., Karwowski E., Toporowski J. (eds) *Economic Crisis and Political Economy.* Palgrave Studies in the History of Economic Thought Series. Palgrave Macmillan, London.

Laski, K. and Podkaminer, L. 2011. Common monetary policy with uncommon wage policies: Centrifugal forces tearing the euro area apart. Intervention. *European Journal of Economics and Economic Policies,* 8(1), 21-29.

Laski, K. and Podkaminer, L. 2012. The basic paradigms of EU economic policy-making need to be changed. *Cambridge Journal of Economics,* 36(1), 253-270.

Laski, K. and Podkaminer, L. 2013. Net private savings in relation to the government's financial balance. In: *Post-Keynesian Views of the Crisis and its Remedies* (Dejuán, Ó., Paños, E. F. and González, J. U. (Eds.)), London: Routledge.

Laver, M. and Shepsle, K. A. 1999. Understanding Government Survival: Empirical Exploration or Analytical Models? *British Journal of Political Science,* 29(2), 395-401.

Lawrence, K. S 2009. The Thermodynamics of Unequal Exchange. *International Journal of Comparative Sociology,* 50(3-4), 335-359.

Levine, R. E. and Renelt, D. 1992. Sensitivity Analysis of Cross-Country Growth Regressions. *The American Economic Review,* 82(4), 942-963.

Longo, F. 2008. Quality of governance: Impartiality is not enough. *Governance. An International Journal of Policy Administration and Institutions.* 21(2): 191-196.

Longo, S. and York, R. 2008. Agricultural Exports and the Environment: A Cross-National Study of Fertilizer and Pesticide Consumption. *Rural Sociology,* 73(1), 82-104.

Mahutga, M. C. and Bandelji, N. 2008. Foreign Investment and Income Inequality: The Natural Experiment of Central and Eastern Europe. *International Journal of Comparative Sociology,* 49(6), 429-454.

Mandelbaum, K. 1945. *The industrialisation of backward areas by K. Mandelbaum, assisted by J. R. L. Schneider.* Oxford: B. Blackwell.

Mankiw, N. G., Romer, D. and Weil, D. N. 1992. A Contribution to the Empirics of Economic Growth. *Quarterly Journal of Economics,* 107(2), 407-437.

Martin, P. and Straubhaar, T. 2002. Best practices to reduce migration pressures. *International Migration,* 40(3): 5-23.

Massey, D. S. et al. 1993. Theories of International Migration: A Review and Appraisal. *Population and Development Review,* 19(3): 431-466.

Matsuyama, K. 1992. Agricultural productivity, comparative advantage, and economic growth. *Journal of Economic Theory,* 58 (2), pp. 317-334.

Matt, A. 2010. Good Government Means Different Things in Different Countries. *Governance. An International Journal of Policy Administration and Institutions.* 23(1): 7-35.

Mazumdar, K. 1996. An analysis of causal flow between social development and economic growth: The social development index. *American Journal of Economics and Sociology,* 55(3): 361-383.

Mazumdar, K. 2000. Causal flow between human well-being and per capita real gross domestic product. *Social Indicators Research,* 50(3): 297-313.

McCleary, R. M. and Barro, R. J. 2006. Religion and economy. *The Journal of Economic Perspectives,* 20(2), 49-72.

McCleary, R. M. and Barro, R. J. 2006. Religion and political economy in an international panel. *Journal for the Scientific study of religion,* 45(2), 149-175.

McDowell, L. 1992. Doing Gender. Feminism, Feminists and Research Methods in Human Geography. *Transactions of the Institute of British Geographers,* 17(4): 399-416.

McKibbin, W. J. and Fernando, R. 2020. *The global macroeconomic impacts of COVID-19: Seven scenarios.* CAMA, Centre for Applied Macroeconomic Analysis, CAMA Working Paper 19/2020, February 2020.

Meadows, D. H. 1992. Smart development, not dumb growth. *Technology Review,* 95(6): 68-89.

Mintz, A. and Stevenson, R. T. 1995. Defense expenditures, economic growth, and the peace-dividend. A longitudinal analysis of 103 countries. *Journal of Conflict Resolution,* 39(2): 283-305.

Molle, W. and Boeckhout, S. 1995. Economic disparity under conditions of integration. A long term view of the European case. *Papers in Regional Science,* 74(2): 105-123.

Moon, B. E. and Dixon, W. J. 1992. Basic Needs and Growth Welfare Trade-Offs. *International Studies Quarterly,* 36(2): 191-212.

Mostafa, M. M. 2010a. A Bayesian approach to analyzing the ecological footprint of 140 nations. *Ecological Indicators,* 10(4), 808-817.

Mostafa, M. M. 2010b. Clustering the ecological footprint of nations using Kohonens self-organizing maps. *Expert Systems with Applications,* 37(4), 2747-2755.

Mostafa, M. M. and Nataraajan, R. 2009. A neuro-computational intelligence analysis of the ecological footprint of nations. *Computational Statistics and Data Analysis,* 53(9), 3516-3531.

Müller, G. P. and Bornschier, V. 1988. *Comparative world data: a statistical handbook for social science.* Baltimore: Johns Hopkins University Press.

Newman, B. A. and Thomson, R. J. 1989. Economic Growth and Social Development. A Longitudinal Analysis of Causal Priority. *World Development,* 17(4): 461-471.

Ng, Y. -K. 2008a. Environmentally responsible happy nation index: Towards an internationally acceptable national success indicator. *Social Indicators Research,* (85), 3: 425-446.

Ng, Y. -K. 2008b. Happiness studies: Ways to improve comparability and some public policy implications. *Economic Record,* 84, June: 253-266.

Nugent, C. and Shandra, J. M. 2009. State Environmental Protection Efforts, Womens Status, and World Polity. A Cross-National Analysis. *Organization & Environment,* 22(3), 293-310.

Orloff, A. 1996. Gender in the welfare state. *Annual Review of Sociology,* 22: 51-78.

Oswald, A. J. 1997. Happiness and economic performance. *Economic Journal,* 107(445): 1815-1831.

Paya, I., Venetis, I. A., Peel, D. A. 2003. Further evidence on PPP adjustment speeds: The case of effective real exchange rates and the EMS. *Oxford Bulletin of Economics and Statistics,* 65(4): 421-437.

Poe, S. C. and Tate, C. N. 1994. Repression of Human Rights to Personal Integrity in the 1980s. A Global Analysis. *American Political Science Review,* 88(4): 853-872.

Pollin, R. 1998. The" reserve army of labor" and the "natural rate of unemployment": Can Marx, Kalecki, Friedman, and Wall Street all be wrong?. *Review of Radical Political Economics,* 30(3), 1-13.

Popper, K. S. 2012. *The open society and its enemies.* Routledge.

Potrafke, N. 2015. The evidence on globalisation. *World Economy,* 38 (3), pp. 509-552. doi: 10.1111/twec.12174.

Poza, E. 1989. *Smart growth: critical choices for business continuity and prosperity.* San Francisco: Jossey-Bass.

Prebisch, R. 1950. *The economic development of Latin America and its principal problems.* Economic Commission for Latin America, New York: United Nations Department of Economic Affairs.

Prebisch, R. 1983. The crisis of capitalism and international trade *ECLAC Review/Revista de la CEPAL (Santiago),* 20, August: 51 - 74.

Prebisch, R. 1988. Dependence, development, and interdependence. In: G. Ranis and T. P. Schultz (Eds.). *The State of Development Economics,* 31 - 41. Oxford, United Kingdom: Basil Blackwell, 1988.

Ram, R. 1982. Composite Indices of Physical Quality of Life, Basic Needs Fulfillment, and Income. A Principal Component Representation. *Journal of Development Economics,* 11(2): 227-247.

Ram, R. 1986. Government Size and Economic Growth. A New Framework and Some Evidence from Cross-Section and Time-Series Data. *American Economic Review,* 76(1): 191-203.

Ram, R. 1997. Tropics and development: an empirical investigation. *World Development,* 25(9): 1443-1452.

Rankin, K. N. 2002. Social capital, microfinance, and the politics of development. *Feminist Economics,* 8(1): 1-24.

Rennstich, J. 2007. Is Globalization self-organizing? In: G. Modelski, T. C. Devezas, W. R. Thompson (Eds.)). *Globalization as Evolutionary Process. Modeling Global Change,* 74 – 107. London and New York: Routledge.

Reuveny, R. and Li Q. 2003. Economic Openness, Democracy, and Income Inequality: An Empirical Analysis. *Comparative Political Studies,* 36(5), 575-601.

Reuveny, R. and Thompson, W. W. 2004. World Economic Growth, Systemic Leadership, and Southern Debt Crises. *Journal of Peace Research,* 41(1) 5-24.

Rodriguez, F. and Rodrik, D. 2001. Trade policy and economic growth: A sceptics guide to the cross-national evidence. In Bernanke, B. S. and

Rogoff, K., Editors, *NBER Macroeconomics Annual 2000.* Cambridge, MA: MIT Press.

Rodríguez, F., and Rodrik, D. 2000. Trade policy and economic growth: A skeptic's guide to the cross-national evidence. *NBER Macroeconomics Annual,* 15 (1), pp. 228-325.

Rodrik, D. 2006. Goodbye Washington Consensus, Hello Washington Confusion? A Review of the World Bank's Economic Growth in the 1990s: Learning from a Decade of Reform. *Journal of Economic Literature,* 44, 2006: 973-987.

Rodrik, D., Subramanian, A., Trebbi, F. 2004. Institutions rule: The primacy of institutions over geography and integration in economic development. *Journal of Economic Growth,* 9(2): 131-165.

Rondinelli, D. A. 1987. Export processing zones and economic development in Asia. A review and reassessment of a means of promoting growth and jobs. *American Journal of Economics and Sociology,* 46(1): 89-105.

Rosenstein-Rodan, P. N. 1964. *Capital formation and economic development.* London: Allen & Unwin.

Ross, R. J. S. 2004. *Slaves to Fashion. Poverty and Abuse in the New Sweatshops.* Ann Arbor: University of Michigan Press.

Rothschild, K. W. 1944. The Small Nation and World Trade. *The Economic Journal,* April: 26 - 40.

Rothschild, K. W. 1954. *The theory of wages.* Oxford: Blackwell.

Rothschild, K. W. 1957. Der Lohnanteil am Gesamteinkommen: einige Bemerkungen zu einem umstrittenen Problem [The wage share of total income: a few comments on a controversial issue]. *Weltwirtschaftliches Archiv,* 78 (2), 157 – 202.

Rothschild, K. W. 1958. Einkommensbildung und Einkommensverteilung [Income generation and income distribution]. *Weltwirtschaftliches Archiv,* 80 (2), 53 – 58.

Rothschild, K. W. 1959. The limitations of economic growth models. *Kyklos,* 12 (4), 567-588.

Rothschild, K. W. 1964. Surveys of foreign postwar developments in economic thought. *The American economic review,* 54 (2), 1 – 55.

Rothschild, K. W. 1965. Theme and variations, remarks on the Kaldorian distribution formula. *Kyklos,* 18 (4), 652 – 669.

Rothstein, B. and Teorell, J. 2008. What is quality of government? A theory of impartial government institutions. *Governance. An International Journal of Policy Administration and Institutions.* 21(2): 165-190.

Rubinson, R. 1976. The World Economy and the Distribution of Income within States – a Cross-national Study. *American Sociological Review,* 41 (4), 638 – 659.

Rudra, N. 2009. Why International Organizations Should Bring Basic Needs Back in. *International Studies Perspectives,* 10(2): 129-150.

Sachs, J. D., and Warner, A. M. 1997. Sources of slow growth in African economies. *Journal of African Economies,* 6 (3), pp. 335-376.

Sala-I-Martin X., Doppelhofer, G. and Miller, R. I. 2004., Determinants of Long-Term Growth: A Bayesian Averaging of Classical Estimates (BACE) Approach. *American Economic Review,* 94(4), 813-835.

Sala-i-Martin, X. 1997. I Just Ran Two Million Regressions The American Economic Review, 87(2), *Papers and Proceedings of the Hundred and Fourth Annual Meeting of the American Economic Association,* May, 1997, 178-183.

Samuelson, P. 1964. Theoretical Notes on Trade Problems. *Review of Economics and Statistics,* 46, 145-154.

Sanderson, M. 2010. International Migration and Human Development in Destination Countries: A Cross-National Analysis of Less-Developed Countries, 1970-2005. *Social Indicators Research,* 96(1), 59-83.

Sanderson, M. R. and Kentor, J. 2008. Foreign Direct Investment and International Migration: A Cross-National Analysis of Less-Developed Countries, 1985-2000. *International Sociology,* 23(4), 514-539.

Sanderson, M. R. and Kentor, J. D. 2009. ,Globalization, Development and International Migration: A Cross-National Analysis of Less-Developed Countries, 1970-2000. *Social Forces,* 88(1), 301-336.

Scanlan, S. 2004. Women, Food Security, and Development in Less-Industrialized Societies: Contributions and Challenges for the New Century. *World Development,* 32(11), 1807-1829.

Schulmeister, S. 2012. *EU-Fiskalpakt: Strangulierung von Wirtschaft und Sozialstaat* [EU Fiscal Compact: Strangling the economy and the welfare state]. Online: http://stephan. schulmeister. wifo. ac. at/fileadmin/homepage_schulmeister/files/Fiskalpakt_Misere__end_04 _12. pdf [12.01. 2014].

Schulmeister, S. 2012. Vorwärts in die 1930er Jahre? [Forward to the 1930s?]. *WSI-Mitteilungen,* 65(6), 404-404.

Schulmeister, S. 2014. *Der Fiskalpakt-Hauptkomponente einer Systemkrise* [*The main component of a systemic crisis in the Fiscal Compact*] (No. 480). WIFO Working Papers.

Schulmeister, S. 2018. Das Richtige im Falschen: Verteidigen wir den Euro! [Right for wrong: let's defend the euro!]. *Blätter für deutsche und internationale Politik,* 7(2018), 51-62. https://www.blaetter.de/ausgabe/2018/juli/das-richtige-im-falschen-verteidigen-wir-den-euro.

Schumacher, E. F. 1973a. *Small is beautiful; Economics as if people mattered.* New York: Harper & Row.

Schumacher, E. F. 1973b. Western Europe's Energy Crisis: A Problem of Life-Styles. *Ambio,* Vol. 2(6): 228-232.

Schumacher, E. F. 1976. Patterns of Human Settlement. *Ambio,* 5(3): 91-97.

Schumacher, E. F. 1977. *A guide for the perplexed.* New York: Harper & Row.

Schumpeter, J. A. 1908. *Wesen und Hauptinhalt der theoretischen Nationalökonomie.* Leipzig: Duncker & Humblot. [*The Nature and Essence of Economic Theory*]. Rutgers, New Jersey: Transaction Publishers, 2009].

Schumpeter, J. A. 1912. *Theorie der wirtschaftlichen Entwicklung.* Leipzig: Duncker & Humblot [*The Theory of economic development: an inquiry into profits, capital, credit, interest and the business cycle/ by Joseph A. Schumpeter; translated from the German by Redvers Opie.* Cambridge (Mass.): Harvard University Press, 1934].

Schumpeter, J. A. 1939. *Business cycles. A theoretical, historical, and statistical analysis of the capitalist process.* New York, London: McGraw-Hill Book Company.

Schumpeter, J. A. 1942. *The Process of Creative Destruction.* London: Unwin.

Schumpeter, J. A. 1950. *Capitalism, Socialism and Democracy.* New York & London: Harper & Row.

Schumpeter, J. A. 1950. *Capitalism, Socialism and Democracy.* New York & London: Harper & Row.

Schumpeter, J. A. 1954. *History of economic analysis.* New York: Oxford University Press.

Seers, D. and Öström, K. (Eds.) 1983. *The Crises of the European regions.* London: Macmillan in association with the European Association of Development Institutes.

Seers, D. Ed. 1981. *Dependency theory: a critical reassessment.* London: Pinter.

Seers, D., Schaffer, B. and Kiljunen, M.-L. 1979. *Underdeveloped Europe: studies in core-periphery relations.* Atlantic Highlands, N.J.: Humanities Press.

Seers, D., Vaitsos C, with the assistance of Marja-Liisa Kiljunen 1980. *Integration and unequal development: The experience of the EEC.* London: Macmillan.

Selden, T. M. and Song, D. Q. 1994. Environmental quality and development. Is there are Kuznets curve for air pollution emissions? *Journal of Environmental Economics and Management,* 27(2): 147-162.

Sen, A. 2003. Missing women—revisited. *British Medical Journal,* 327 (7427), pp. 1297-1298.

Shandra, J. M. 2007a. Economic dependency, repression, and deforestation: A quantitative, cross-national analysis. *Sociological Inquiry,* 77(4), 543-571.

Shandra, J. M. 2007b. International Nongovernmental Organizations and Deforestation: Good, Bad, or Irrelevant? *Social Science Quarterly,* 88(3), 665-689.

Shandra, J. M., Leckband, C. and London, B. 2009. Ecologically Unequal Exchange and Deforestation: A Cross-National Analysis of Forestry Export Flows. *Organization & Environment,* 22(2), 208-229.

Shandra, J. M., Leckband, Ch., McKinney, L. A., and London, B. 2009. Ecologically Unequal Exchange, World Polity, and Biodiversity Loss. A Cross-National Analysis of Threatened Mammals. *International Journal of Comparative Sociology,* 50(3-4), 285-310.

Shandra, J. M., London B., Whooley, O. P. and Williamson, J. B. 2004. International Nongovernmental Organizations and Carbon Dioxide Emissions in the Developing World: A Quantitative, Cross-National Analysis. *Sociological Inquiry,* 74(4), 520-545.

Shandra, J. M., London, B., and Williamson, J. B. 2003. Environmental Degradation, Environmental Sustainability, and Overurbanization in the Developing World: A Quantitative, Cross-National Analysis. *Sociological Perspectives,* 46(3), 309-329.

Shandra, J. M., Nobles, J. E., London, B., and Williamson, J. B 2005. Multinational Corporations, Democracy and Child Mortality: A Quantitative, Cross-National Analysis of Developing Countries. *Social Indicators Research,* 73(2), 267-293.

Shandra, J. M., Nobles, J., London, B., and Williamson, J. B. 2004. Dependency, Democracy, and Infant Mortality: A Quantitative, Cross-National Analysis of Less Developed Countries. *Social Science & Medicine,* 59(2), 321-333.

Shandra, J. M., Shandra, C. L. and London, B. 2008. Women, non-governmental organizations, and deforestation: a cross-national study. *Population and Environment,* 30(1-2), 48-72.

Shandra, J. M., Shandra, C. L. and London, B. 2010. Do Non-Governmental Organizations Impact Health? A Cross-National Analysis of Infant Mortality. *International Journal of Comparative Sociology,* 51(1-2), 137-164.

Shandra, J. M., Shor, E. and London, B. 2009. World Polity, Unequal Ecological Exchange, and Organic Water Pollution: A Cross-National Analysis of Developing Nations. *Human Ecology Review,* 16(1), 53-63.

Shandra, J. M., Shor, E. and London, Bruce 2008. Debt, Structural Adjustment, and Organic Water Pollution. *Organization & Environment,* 21(1), 38-55.

Singa Boyenge, J. -P. 2007. *ILO database on export processing zones* (Revised), WP. 251; Sectoral Activities Programme; Working Paper; International Labour Office; Geneva, April 2007.

Singa Boyenge, J-P 2007. *ILO database on export processing zones.* (Revised). WP.251; Sectoral Activities Programme; Working Paper; International Labour Office; Geneva, April 2007.

Singer, H. W. 1975. *The strategy of international development: essays in the economics of backwardness.* H. W. Singer; edited by Alec Cairncross and Mohinder Puri. London: Macmillan.

Singer, H. W. and Ansari, J. A. 1988. *Rich and poor countries: consequences of international economic disorder.* London; Boston: Unwin Hyman.

Singer, H. W. and Roy, S. 1993. *Economic progress and prospects in the Third World: lessons of development experience since 1945.* Aldershot, England; Brookfield, Vt., USA: E. Elgar.

Singh, R. D. 1985. State intervention, foreign economic aid, savings and growth in LDCs. Some Recent Evidence. *Kyklos,* 38(2): 216-232.

Skaggs, K. A. S. 2010. Implications of emerging neoliberal politics on conservation governance in the South Carolina Low country. *Masters Abstracts International,* vol. 48, no. 06, pp. 3385.

Solomon, H. and Tausch, A. 2020. *Islamism, crisis and democratization: Implications of the World Values Survey for the Muslim world (Perspectives on development in the Middle East and North Africa (Mena region).* Cham: Springer.

Solomon, H. and Tausch, A. 2021. *Arab MENA countries: Vulnerabilities and constraints against democracy on the eve of the global Covid-19 crisis.* (Perspectives on development in the Middle East and North Africa (Mena region)). Cham: Springer.

Stavins, R. N., 2002. *Experience with Market-Based Environmental Policy Instruments.* FEEM Working Paper No. 52. 2002; KSG Working Paper No. 00-004. Available at SSRN: http://ssrn.com/abstract=199848 or doi:10. 2139/ssrn. 199848.

Steindl, J. 1952. *Maturity and Stagnation in American Capitalism.* Oxford: Basil Blackwell.

Steindl, J. 1979. Stagnation theory and stagnation policy. *Cambridge Journal of Economics,* 1979(3), 1-14.

Steindl, J. 1988. Diskussionsbeitrag zur EG-Frage [Contribution to the discussion on the EC question]. *Kurswechsel,* 4 (3), pp. 3–7.

Steindl, J. 1990. *Economic Papers 1941-88.* Basingstoke: MacMillan.

Stern, D. I. 2004. The rise and fall of the environmental Kuznets curve. *World Development,* 32(8): 1419-1439.

Stern, D. I., Common, M. S. and Barbier, E. B. 1996. Economic growth and environmental degradation: The environmental Kuznets curve and sustainable development. *World Development,* 24(7): 1151-1160.

Stevenson, B. and Wolfers, J. 2008. Economic Growth and Subjective Well-Being: Reassessing the Easterlin Paradox. *IZA Discussion Paper Series,* IZA DP No. 3654, IZA Bonn, available at: http://ftp.iza.org/dp3654.pdf

Stockhammer, E. 2008. Is the NAIRU theory a monetarist, new Keynesian, post Keynesian or a Marxist theory?. *Metroeconomica*, 59(3), 479-510.

Stockhammer, E., Constantine, C. and Reissl, S. 2020. Explaining the euro crisis: Current account imbalances, credit booms and economic policy in different economic paradigms. *Journal of Post Keynesian Economics,* 1-36.

Sunkel, O. (Ed.) 2003. *Development from within: toward a neostructuralist approach for Latin America.* Boulder, CO: L. Rienner.

Sunkel, O. 1966. The Structural Background of Development Problems in Latin America. *Weltwirtschaftliches Archive,* 97(1), 22 – 63.

Sunkel, O. 1973. Transnational capitalism and national disintegration in Latin America. *Social and Economic Studies,* 22 (1), 132 - 76.

Sunkel, O. 1978. The Development of Development Thinking. In: J. J. Villamil (Ed.) *Transnational Capitalism and National Development. New Perspectives on Dependence,* 19 - 30, Hassocks, Sussex: Harvester Press.

Sylwester, K. 2000. Income inequality, education expenditures, and growth. *Journal of Development Economics,* 63(2): 379-398.

Taubenberger, J. K. and Morens, D. M. 2006. 1918 Influenza: the mother of all pandemics. *Emerging infectious diseases,* 12(1), 15.

Tausch, A. 2003. Social Cohesion, Sustainable Development and Turkey's Accession to the European Union: Implications from a Global Model. *Alternatives. Turkish Journal of International Relations,* Vol. 2(1), 2003.

Tausch, A. 2005. Is Islam really a development blockade? *Insight Turkey,* vol. 7(1), 124-135, Jan-Mar.

Tausch, A. 2007. Quantitative World System Studies Contradict Current Islamophobia: World Political Cycles, Global Terrorism, and World Development. *Alternatives: Turkish Journal of International Relations,* vol. 6(1)-2, 15-81, spring-summer 2007. .

Tausch, A. 2007. War Cycles' *Social Evolution and History (Moscow),* 6 (2), 39 – 74.

Tausch, A. 2008. Разрушительное созидание? (Рассуждения в духе Шумпетера о некоторых трендах и Лиссабонском процессе в Европе) [Destructive Creation' (Schumpeter-Style Reasonings on Some Trends and Lisbon Process in Europe)]. *Mirovaja ekonomika i meždunarodnyje otnošenija,* (Moscow). 10, 2008, 34 – 41.

Tausch, A. 2010. 'Dataset for 'Globalization, the human condition and sustainable development in the 21st Century. Cross-national perspectives and European implications'' available at http://www.hichemkaroui.com/?p=2383 *Social Sciences and Humanities – MESOJ (Middle East Studies Online Journal - ISSN 2109-9618)* - (2010) Volume 1 No 2.

Tausch, A. 2010. Globalisation and development: the relevance of classical "dependency" theory for the world today. *International Social Science Journal,* 61(202), 467-488.

Tausch, A. 2012. A globalization-oriented perspective on health, inequality and socio-economic development. *The International journal of health planning and management,* 27(1), 2-33.

Tausch, A. 2012. *International Macroquantitative Data. Faculty of Economics,* Corvinus University of Budapest, available at http://www.uni-corvinus.hu/index.php?id=47854&tx_ttnews%5Btt_news%5D=0&tx_ttnews%5BbackPid%5D=31638&tx_ttnews%5Bcale

ndarYear%5D=2012&tx_ttnews%5BcalendarMonth%5D=6&cHash=a f8ef6888f7c9922b83b113f71c1ca32.

Tausch, A. 2019. Migration from the Muslim world to the West: Its most recent trends and effects. *Jewish Political Studies Review,* 30(1-2), 65-225, available at http://jcpa.org/article/migration-from-the-muslim-world-to-the-west-its-most-recent-trends-and-effects/ (with data definitions and sources). Free data download available from https://www.academia.edu/37568941/Migration_from_the_Muslim_World_to_the_West_Its_Most_Recent_Trends_and_Effects.

Tausch, A. and Ghymers, Ch. 2006. *From the Washington towards a Vienna Consensus? A quantitative analysis on globalization, development and global governance.* Hauppauge NY: Nova Science.

Tausch, A. and Heshmati, A. (2012) *Globalization, the human condition and sustainable development in the twenty-first century: Cross-national perspectives and European implications.* https://www.scopus.com/inward/record.uri?eid=2-s2.0-84939789242&doi=10.7135%2fUPO9780857286550&partnerID=40&md5=32618c3ba9b7101853ea357f86de2703. doi: 10.7135/UPO9780857286550. London, New York, and Delhi: Anthem Press.

Tausch, A. and Heshmati, A. 2012. The Effects of Multinational Corporation (MNC) Penetration on the Global Political Economy. A Re-analysis of a Recurrent Sociological Proposition with Contemporary Data. *Sociologia,* 44(3), 314-347.

Tausch, A. and Heshmati, A. 2013. *Globalization, the human condition, and sustainable development in the twenty-first century: cross-national perspectives and European implications.* London, New York and Delhi: Anthem Press (with data definitions and sources). Free data download available from https://www.academia.edu/35044095/Globalization_the_human_condition_and_sustainable_development_in_the_21st_Century._Cross-national_perspectives_and_European_implications_Codebook_and_EXCEL_data_file.

Tausch, A. and Prager, F. 1993. *Towards a Socio-Liberal Theory of World Development.* Basingstoke and New York: Palgrave Macmillan/St. Martins Press.

Taylor, A. M. 1992. External dependence, demographic burdens, and Argentine economic decline after the *Belle Epoque. Journal of Economic History,* 52(4): 907-936.

Taylor, J. E. 1999. The new economics of labour migration and the role of remittances in the migration process. *International Migration,* 37(1): 63-88.

Taylor, J. E. 2006. International Migration and Economic Development. UN/POP/MIG/SYMP/2006/09, 26 June 2006, *International Symposium on International Migration and Development,* Population Division, Department of Economic and Social Affairs, United Nations Secretariat, Turin, Italy, 28-30 June 2006, available at: http://www.un.org/esa/population/migration/turin/Symposium_Turin_files/P09_SYMP_Taylor.pdf.

Tsai, P.-L. 1995. Foreign direct investment and income inequality: Further evidence. *World Development,* 23 (3), 469-483.

UNDP (current issues). *United Nations Human Development Report.* Available at http://www.hdr.undp.org/.

United Nations Conference on Trade and Development 2009. *World Investment Report.* New York and Geneva: United Nations.

United Nations Economic Commission for Latin America, ECLAC/CEPAL, 2002. *Globalización y desarrollo.* available at: http://www.eclac.cl/cgi-bin/getProd.asp?xml=/publicaciones/xml/6/10026/P10026.xml&xsl=/tpl/p9f.xsl&base=/MDG/tpl/top-bottom.xsl.

Ursúa, J. F. 2010. "*Long-Run Volatility*," Harvard University, unpublished. Available at: http://www.people.fas.harvard.edu/~jfursua/papers.html.

Ursúa, J. F. 2010. "*Macroeconomic Archaeology: Unearthing Crises and Long-Run Trends*," Harvard University, available at: http://www.people.fas.harvard.edu/~jfursua/papers.html.

Veenhoven, R. 1996. Happy Life-expectancy. A comprehensive measure of quality-of-life in nations. *Social Indicators Research,* (39), 1-58.

Wallerstein, I. 2000. *The Essential Wallerstein.* New York: The New Press.

Weede, E. 1980. Beyond Misspecification in Sociological Analyses of Income Inequality. *American Sociological Review,* 45, 497-501.

Weede, E. 1981a. Dependency Theories and Economic Growth: A Cross-National Study. *Koelner Zeitschrift fur Soziologie und Sozialpsychologie*, 33(4), 690-707.

Weede, E. 1981b. Militär, Multis und Wirtschaft [Military, multis and economy]. *Schweizerische Zeitschrift für Soziologie/Revue Suisse de sociologie,* 7(1): 113-127.

Weede, E. 1983. Military Participation Ratio. Human Capital Formation and Economic Growth: A Cross-National Analysis. *Journal of Political and Military Sociology,* 11:11-29.

Weede, E. 1985. *Entwicklungsländer in der Weltgesellschaft* [*Developing countries in world society*]. Opladen: Westdeutscher Verlag.

Weede, E. 1986. Rent Seeking, Military Participation and Economic Performance in LDCs. *Journal of Conflict Resolution.* 30:291-314.

Weede, E. 1993. The Impact of Military Participation on Economic Growth and Income Inequality: Some New Evidence. *Journal of Political and Military Sociology,* 21:241-258.

Weede, E. 2002. Impact of Intelligence and Institutional Improvements on Economic Growth. *Kyklos,* 55 (3), 361 - 380.

Weede, E. 2004. Does Human Capital Strongly Affect Economic Growth Rates? Yes, But Only If Assessed Properly. *Comparative Sociology,* 3 (2), 115 - 134.

Weede, E. and Jagodzinski W. 1980. Weltpolitische und ökonomische Determinanten einer ungleichen Einkommensverteilung. Eine international vergleichende Studie [World political and economic determinants of an unequal income distribution. An international comparative study]. *Zeitschrift für Soziologie,* 9, 132-148.

Weede, E. and Kampf, S. 2002. The impact of intelligence and institutional improvements on economic growth. *Kyklos,* 55(3): 361-380.

Weede, E. and Tiefenbach, H. 1980a. Correlates of the Size Distribution of Income in Cross-National Analyses. *Journal of Politics,* 43(4), 1029-1041.

Weede, E. and Tiefenbach, H. 1980b. Some Recent Explanations of Income Inequality: An Evaluation and Critique. *International Studies Quarterly,* 25, 255-282.

Weede, E. and Tiefenbach, H. 1981. Three Dependency Explanations of Economic Growth: A Critical Evaluation. *European Journal of Political Research,* 9(4), 391-406.

Wilkinson, R. G. 1992. For Debate – Income Distribution and Life Expectancy. *British Medical Journal, BMJ,* 304, 6820: 165-168.

Wilkinson, R. G. 1997. Socioeconomic determinants of health - Health inequalities: Relative or absolute material standards? *British Medical Journal, BMJ,* 314, 7080: 591-595, published February 22, 1997.

Wilkinson, R. G. and Picket K. E. 2006. Income inequality and population health: A review and explanation of the evidence. *British Medical Journal, BMJ,* 62 (7): 1768-1784, April.

Williamson, J. A. 2002. *Is Protection Bad for Growth? Will Globalization Last? Looking for Answers in History.* Presented at the 13th IEHA Congress, Buenos Aires, August 22-26, 2002 Draft Date: June 2002. Available at: http://www.economics.harvard.edu/faculty/williamson/jwilliamworkingpapers (download: August 1, 2011).

World Bank. 2005. *Economic Growth in the 1990s: Learning from a Decade of Reform.* Washington, DC.: World Bank.

Wu, J., Cai, W., Watkins, D. and Glanz J. 2020. How the Virus Got Out. March 22, 2020, *New York Times*, available at https://www.nytimes.com/interactive/2020/03/22/world/coronavirus-spread.html.

York, R., Rosa, E. A. and Dietz, T. 2003. Footprints on the earth: The environmental consequences of modernity. *American Sociological Review,* 68(2): 279-300.

Zak, P. J. and Knack, S. 2001. Trust and growth. *The economic journal,* 111(470), 295-321.

Ziesemer, T. H. W. 2009. Worker Remittances and Growth: The Physical and Human Capital Channels. *Jahrbuecher fuer Nationaloekonomie und Statistik,* 229(6): 743-773.

ABOUT THE AUTHOR

Arno Tausch
Adjunct Professor of Political Science at Innsbruck University
Associate Professor of Economics, Corvinus University, Budapest

Arno Tausch is currently Honorary Associate Professor of Economics, Corvinus University, Budapest, Hungary (since Fall Semester 2010) and Adjunct Professor (Universitaetsdozent) of Political Science at Innsbruck University, Department of Political Science, Innsbruck University, Austria (since 1988). He authored or co-authored books and articles for major international publishers and journals, among them 22 books in English, 2 books in French, 8 books in German, and currently 110 articles in peer-reviewed journals and also numerous press articles in the media of several countries

INDEX

D

E

R

S

T

U

V

W

Y

Z